Blockchain for Decision Makers

A systematic guide to using blockchain for improving your business

Romain Tormen

BIRMINGHAM - MUMBAI

Blockchain for Decision Makers

Commissioning Editor: Sunith Shetty
Acquisition Editor: Yogesh Deokar
Content Development Editor: Athikho Sapuni Rishana
Senior Editor: Sofi Rogers
Technical Editor: Manikandan Kurup
Copy Editor: Safis Editing
Project Coordinator: Kirti Pisat
Proofreader: Safis Editing
Indexer: Priyanka Dhadke
Production Designer: Aparna Bhagat

First published: September 2019

Production reference: 1260919

Published by Packt Publishing Ltd.
Livery Place
35 Livery Street
Birmingham
B3 2PB, UK.

ISBN 978-1-83855-227-5

www.packt.com

Packt.com

Subscribe to our online digital library for full access to over 7,000 books and videos, as well as industry leading tools to help you plan your personal development and advance your career. For more information, please visit our website.

Why subscribe?

- Spend less time learning and more time coding with practical eBooks and Videos from over 4,000 industry professionals

- Improve your learning with Skill Plans built especially for you

- Get a free eBook or video every month

- Fully searchable for easy access to vital information

- Copy and paste, print, and bookmark content

Did you know that Packt offers eBook versions of every book published, with PDF and ePub files available? You can upgrade to the eBook version at www.packt.com and as a print book customer, you are entitled to a discount on the eBook copy. Get in touch with us at customercare@packtpub.com for more details.

At www.packt.com, you can also read a collection of free technical articles, sign up for a range of free newsletters, and receive exclusive discounts and offers on Packt books and eBooks.

Contributors

About the author

Romain Tormen is a senior consultant for PwC, a worldwide consulting firm. He has experience of digital transformation within a variety of industries and business units. Specializing in emerging technologies, he promotes the use of blockchain to his clients from the perspective of improved transaction security, transparency, disintermediation, and third-party authentication. He is a contributing writer to one of the most widely read, tech-oriented websites – hackernoon. Romain offers business insights and provides use cases for a broad range of industries.

About the reviewers

Narendranath Reddy is an experienced full stack blockchain engineer and Hyperledger Fabric expert with a proven track record of helping enterprises to build production-ready, blockchain-backed applications. He is an experienced innovator and creative thinker. He has won four hackathons on blockchain and is a keynote speaker, regularly speaking about blockchain and distributed ledgers. He is currently working as a blockchain software engineer at Consensys, Dubai, having previously worked as a blockchain developer at Blockgemini, Dubai, and as a software developer at UST Global, Trivandrum, and Madrid, Spain.

Packt is searching for authors like you

If you're interested in becoming an author for Packt, please visit `authors.packtpub.com` and apply today. We have worked with thousands of developers and tech professionals, just like you, to help them share their insight with the global tech community. You can make a general application, apply for a specific hot topic that we are recruiting an author for, or submit your own idea.

Table of Contents

Preface

Blockchain-based apps, in addition to cryptocurrencies, are being developed in a variety of industries, including banking, the supply chain, and healthcare, in order to achieve digital transformation and enhance the user experience. Blockchain is not only about Bitcoin or cryptocurrencies, but also about different technologies, such as peer-to-peer networks, consensus mechanisms, and cryptography. These technologies together help to sustain trustless environments in which digital value can be transferred between individuals without intermediaries.

This book will help you understand the basics of blockchain, including cryptographic methods, hash functions, and consensus mechanisms. You will then focus on how blockchain is used today in different industries and the technological challenges faced while implementing a blockchain strategy. The book will also enable you, as a decision maker, to understand blockchain from a technical perspective and evaluate its applicability in business. Finally, you'll get to grips with cloud-based solutions and blockchain frameworks, such as Hyperledger and Quorum, and how to use them.

By the end of this book, you will have learned about the current use cases of blockchain and be able to implement a blockchain strategy on your own.

Who this book is for

This book is for CXOs, business professionals, organization leaders, decision makers, technology enthusiasts, and managers who wish to understand how blockchain is implemented in different organizations, its impact, and how it can be customized according to business needs. Prior experience with blockchain is not required.

What this book covers

Chapter 1, *Basics of Blockchain and the Illustration of Village Beta,* aims to provide the reader with a straightforward example in terms of understanding how blockchain truly works and how it can apply to real-life situations. It provides a brief introduction as to why blockchain is a genuine matter for C-level executives and gives an illustration of how it operates.

Chapter 2, *A Technical Dive into Blockchain,* includes a description of the components of blockchain, as well as a description of those stakeholders who compose a blockchain network, before describing a block and its data structure, the hash, the previous hash, the nonce, and the timestamp. We'll then describe hash functions and their role in blockchain as well as discover how cryptography plays an important role in managing identities in the network and identifying stakeholders to provide authentication. We'll introduce symmetric and asymmetric encryption methods and the underlying pairs of keys tied to each account (private and public). We'll explain consensus mechanisms and illustrate the Byzantine Generals Problem, which is the first computer science problem to raise questions regarding consensus in a network in the presence of traitors or faults. We'll eventually go through an explanation of how the network keeps working to achieve truth thanks to game theory and economics.

Chapter 3, *Ethereum and Smart Contracts,* introduces Ethereum, a decentralized platform running like an operating system to build decentralized applications. We'll describe the components of Ethereum, its Ethereum Virtual Machine, which acts as a computer program, its *fuel,* referred to as gas, and its smart contracts, which can trigger actions automatically in respect of their code. We'll explain why Ethereum is so successful, how it differs from Bitcoin, and focus on their underlying consensus mechanisms. We'll finally end the chapter by understanding Ethereum's roadmap to a more scalable and efficient infrastructure and discover a number of real-world applications built on Ethereum.

Chapter 4, *ICOs and Tokenized Fundraising Methods,* explain these new token-based fundraising methods, which generate new cryptocurrencies that are sold against other already existing liquid money. We'll understand the current success of ICOs and why they are so risky, both for investors and project leaders. We'll illustrate a number of ICOs, including Ethereum and the DAO, and differentiate between utility tokens from security tokens as well as introduce legal concerns from regulatory bodies.

Chapter 5, *An Economic and Historical Approach of Blockchain*, provides an economic approach to understanding both Bitcoin and blockchain. It gives historical insights and economic facts to place this new technology in a worldwide context.

Chapter 6, *Blockchain Legality, Compliance, and Regulation*, describes the regulations and the behavior of governments in relation to blockchain, ICOs and cryptocurrencies. While China was initially extremely cautious, the US attempted to legally define ICOs and provide a regulatory framework. Europe is adopting a wait-and-see approach, while there is a genuine need for entrepreneurs to be overseen and helped by public institutions.

Chapter 7, *Blockchain for the Business World and Achievements*, touches upon blockchain applications that have been developed in various industries and use cases that have been conceived. We'll cover several issues, including trustworthiness in official releases, interoperability between IT systems, traceability within supply chains, automation and disintermediation thanks to smart contracts, digital identity management, public and governmental challenges, tokenization in the financial industry, and finally, digital uniqueness. Many fields will be covered throughout this chapter, including retail, healthcare, automotive, luxury goods, manufacturing, shipping, finance, arts, music, and sports.

Chapter 8, *Future Outlook for Blockchain*, describes where blockchain is heading and what can be expected in the near future in terms of the global economy, as well as what enablers blockchain unlocks both for governments and decision makers.

Chapter 9, *Infrastructures and Cloud-Based Solution,* explains what kind of blockchain can be found on the market and how their functionalities have evolved over time. We'll introduce four main blockchain protocols that have been developed to advance enterprise-grade issues and infrastructures available for building a blockchain project. We'll also discover more accessible cloud-based solutions provided by web giants such as Amazon, Microsoft, and IBM.

Chapter 10, *Defining Your Needs*, provides you with a methodology to fulfill a blockchain strategy for your company by defining whether specific business needs could use blockchain as a tool. This chapter also raises important questions and an overview of the costs underlying a blockchain project. In this chapter, you will understand the boundaries in terms of the implementation of a blockchain and whether it is truly a necessity. As a decision maker, you should make pragmatic choices to achieve organic growth and embrace a mindset where becoming digital is only one step to becoming performant and profitable.

To get the most out of this book

This book is primarily intended for decision makers, C-level executives, and any business person willing to grasp the emerging and promising technology that blockchain is. The reader does not need to have specific technical skills or experience as a developer, but instead an ambition to possess the knowledge to understand the blockchain as a whole. What is needed is curiosity and open-mindedness in order to assimilate every piece of information displayed in this book. By the end of the ten chapters, you should be able to appreciate the wide and complex blockchain ecosystem, develop your own opinion, identify relevant use cases for your business, and lead it to success.

It is not mandatory to have an in-depth understanding of the technology before reading this book. However, a degree of familiarity with blockchain would be beneficial. In this regard, this book is beginner-friendly, but requires an important level of curiosity to explore further the different concepts enunciated.

Download the color images

We also provide a PDF file that has color images of the screenshots/diagrams used in this book. You can download it here: `http://www.packtpub.com/sites/default/files/downloads/9781838552275_ColorImages.pdf`.

Conventions used

Bold: Indicates a new term, an important word, or words that you see on screen. For example, words in menus or dialog boxes appear in the text like this. Here is an example: "Select **System info** from the **Administration** panel."

Warnings or important notes appear like this.

Tips and tricks appear like this.

Get in touch

Feedback from our readers is always welcome.

General feedback: If you have questions about any aspect of this book, mention the book title in the subject of your message and email us at customercare@packtpub.com.

Errata: Although we have taken every care to ensure the accuracy of our content, mistakes do happen. If you have found a mistake in this book, we would be grateful if you would report this to us. Please visit www.packtpub.com/support/errata, selecting your book, clicking on the Errata Submission Form link, and entering the details.

Piracy: If you come across any illegal copies of our works in any form on the internet, we would be grateful if you would provide us with the location address or website name. Please contact us at copyright@packt.com with a link to the material.

If you are interested in becoming an author: If there is a topic that you have expertise in, and you are interested in either writing or contributing to a book, please visit authors.packtpub.com.

Reviews

Please leave a review. Once you have read and used this book, why not leave a review on the site that you purchased it from? Potential readers can then see and use your unbiased opinion to make purchase decisions, we at Packt can understand what you think about our products, and our authors can see your feedback on their book. Thank you!

For more information about Packt, please visit packt.com.

Section 1: A First Step into Blockchain and an Exciting World

1

This section provides an explanation and illustration of blockchain, a description of the components of blockchain, and a true understanding of how it works.

This section comprises of the following chapters:

- Chapter 1, *Basics of Blockchain and the Illustration of Village Beta*
- Chapter 2, *A Technical Dive into Blockchain*
- Chapter 3, *Ethereum and Smart Contracts*
- Chapter 4, *ICOs and Tokenized Fundraising Methods*

Basics of Blockchains and the Illustration of Village Beta

1

Blockchain has been pushed into the limelight by a new and controversial form of digital currency called Bitcoin. The success stories of early Bitcoin investors and the launch of Ethereum, a platform allowing the creation of decentralized applications, brought blockchain and cryptocurrencies to the frontier where decision-makers and executives started to pay attention to this emerging piece of technology. Many curious persons began to wonder how it could help them in their personal or professional enterprises, leading them to believe that this innovation could be an appropriate answer to their business issues. The Economist, on October 31, 2015, published the first well-known article about blockchain (`https://www.economist.com/printedition/covers/2015-10-29/ap-e-eu-la-me-na-uk`).

As a decision-maker, being educated enough about new technologies and innovations is paramount for your company to explore and experiment with emerging enablers that will bring competitive advantages and help you to reach a steady growth. Being able to thrive in the digital age is more and more a necessity and a complex task, especially because technological breakthroughs and mass innovation trigger a sharp shift in people's consumption habits, as well as geopolitical challenges and economic changes. Being able to consider, evaluate, and incorporate new technologies to tackle your company's business goals has become critical.

With that in mind, you should be aware that blockchain has the potential to be a paradigm shift that can redesign how organizations operate and how value is shared between economic actors. This disruptive technology is said to change how the world works, how entire industries function, and how value is being exchanged and secured. But, as promising as it is, you must act with caution. We are at the dawn of what blockchain can achieve and it is not a hundred percent mature—it's still being considered an emerging technology.

Throughout this chapter, we will consider an illustration of a blockchain application that will help you to picture and grasp the concepts with ease. By the end of this chapter, you should be able to understand the usability of a blockchain in certain environments and conditions, especially when it comes to exchanging value directly between individuals. You should be able to explain basically how a blockchain works, what are its inner characteristics, and how Bitcoin operates without any central authority.

This chapter includes the following sections:

- The significance of blockchain in the business world
- Understanding blockchains
- Breaking down blockchains

The significance of blockchain in the business world

The latest Gartner's Hype Cycle, published on August 20, 2018, shows how far blockchain is from massive adoption: 5 to 10 years (`https://www.gartner.com/en/newsroom/press-releases/2018-08-20-gartner-identifies-five-emerging-technology-trends-that-will-blur-the-lines-between-human-and-machine`).

The Gartner's Hype Cycle is a visual graphical representation of emerging technologies' maturity and adoption. It is an annual report published by Gartner, an information technology research and consultancy firm.

As stated by Gartner, blockchain has shown many great stories and successful proof of concepts propelled by a wide media coverage and publicity, but still faces many failures and scalability issues. Some products have seen the light, with a real impact on economy and society (Bitcoin and Ethereum are the most well-known) but the mainstream adoption and broad market applicability (the so-called plateau of productivity) will be reached only if products are sustained with large investments and the technology is understood more and more.

According to PwC's 2018 Global Blockchain Survey, 84% of C-level executives report that their organization already has involvement with blockchain technology, but more than 65% of them have not pulled through the pilot stage yet.

The PwC 2018 Global Blockchain Survey was fielded between April and May 2018, surveying 600 executives with technology responsibilities over 15 countries. More than a third of the respondents work in organizations with revenues of $1 billion or greater.

There is a significant misunderstanding around the concept behind blockchain and its applicability within the business world. Cryptocurrencies and blockchain's recent hype makes executives assume that it stands as an answer to every business challenge. In fact, blockchain has to be considered as a layer for securitizing transactions and ensuring transparency of information and authentication of stakeholders in a decentralized environment. Blockchain is often seen as a difficult notion to grasp, especially for non-tech people. This book will help you to identify, as a decision-maker, the opportunities offered by blockchain for you to understand its applicability and ultimately give you the keys for initiating a blockchain project.

Understanding blockchains

Before diving instantly into the technical part, which will be covered in `Chapter 2`, *A Technical Dive into Blockchain*, you should first have an overview of what a blockchain is. If you have already read or heard about the topic, you might have figured out that it is appropriate for any use case relying on trust being ensured by a third party and where value is exchanged between different stakeholders. With the help of a simple example taken from an imaginary situation, the following sections will hopefully unravel the things you might have been confused about and the things you are eager to understand.

Using centralized ledger systems

Imagine a village of 20 people living on an island in the middle of the ocean, without connection to any other tribes or countries. We will call this village, Village Alpha. They live a peaceful life in a resourceful environment where no one lacks anything.

Question: *How do the people of Village Alpha exchange and trade goods and services between each other?*

Avoiding the downsides of bartering, they invent a gold-minted coin, a form of money similar to a dollar bill in today's economy. Because this coin is portable and easy to identify and has a value in the eyes of all of the villagers, it quickly becomes the principal means of payment within the community. To ensure proper trade between each other, they record every exchange in a ledger and appoint one of them as the referring bookkeeper to maintain its accuracy and authenticity. The appointed bookkeeper is rewarded for his/her integrity and honesty by collecting a fee on every transaction.

And that's it! People can buy and sell goods with their gold-minted coins. The truth is ensured by the bookkeeper who keeps the ledger up to date, incentivized to behave fairly by levying fees on transactions. Anyone can challenge him/her by checking the transactions to ascertain proper recording.

The villagers found a solution to their problem, unknowingly inventing the banking system that prevails nowadays.

To keep it simple, I deliberately omitted talk about savings, securities, or gold reserves that are additional components of the nowadays banking system but that are off-topic in our example.

Now, let's assume that the bookkeeper is dishonest. Imagine he/she modifies the ledger during the night and erases some transactions or adds new ones? What if he/she destroys the ledger?

You can see that this system has its shortcomings. The villagers are currently using what we call a centralized payment system where everyone relies on the bookkeeper to ensure the truth.

In our modern society, the bank plays the role of the bookkeeper. When you send money to a friend, you trust the bank to carry out the correct fund transfers

The bank is a trusted third entity that ensures correct financial transactions from one account to another and records them in a book of accounts.

This has major downsides:

- A single point of failure: Imagine a storm wipes out the village and the ledger with it.
- A trusted third party that can be dishonest: Imagine the bookkeeper modifies the transactions.

- A double-spending problem, which, however, is not applicable in our example because we assume they exchange physical goods. If the villagers were exchanging digital value, double-spending would have been an issue in the way that they would need an infrastructure to prevent replication of the digital assets. In other words, they would need a means to prevent an asset to be spent twice. More on that later.

The blockchain alternative

So, how does blockchain offer a powerful alternative to this traditional centralized payment system?

Let's take the village on the neighboring island to see how they proceeded from the initial problem of exchanging goods. This village, which we will call Village Beta, is also composed of 20 people.

Instead of electing one of them as the bookkeeper who will certify the truth and the history of transactions between them, they find another solution.

They create a book in which each page is designed as a spreadsheet with ten lines and three columns. The lines will be used to input transactions and the columns to input three pieces of information: the sender's address, the recipient's address, and the amount, as shown in the following diagram:

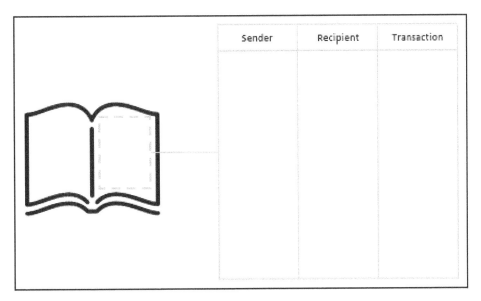

Then, they replicate the book 19 times and hand over one copy to each villager so that everyone possesses one book. Finally, they craft 10,000 coins that they call Villagecoin and distribute 10 to each one of them, leaving the remaining in a vault.

Empowering the ledger

When someone wants to make a transaction, he or she has to go to the central place of the village and shout to everybody else what transaction he or she is willing to make. When hearing the transaction, the other villagers write it down on the first page of their book: Alice gives 2 Villagecoin to Bob, Chuck gives 5 Villagecoin to Dan, and so on. In this way, every transaction is recorded in everyone's book, as shown in the following diagram:

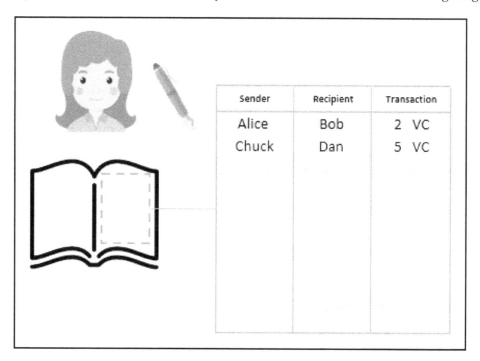

Sender	Recipient	Transaction
Alice	Bob	2 VC
Chuck	Dan	5 VC

With this system, no one was entrusted to assert the accuracy of a central book but instead, everyone is responsible for their own book.

This organization allows two things:

- **Transparency:** The villagers can check whether a villager has enough money. Since all of the transactions are recorded, it's easy to check that Alice cannot send 15 Villagecoin to Dan, since she was given 10 Villagecoin on the first day and then sent 2 Villagecoin to Bob. She has therefore, only 8 Villagecoin remaining.
- **A first level of security:** Since everyone should have the same book and history of transactions, if Alice came to falsify a transaction in her book, it would turn invalid because everyone else (the majority) has the correct transactions recorded. Alice would just end up with an incorrect book and would need to retrieve a valid copy from another villager.

In this example, the book is what we call a **database** (or **ledger**), where all transactions and value transfers are logged. The village is the **community** that empowers the ledger; it is a network infrastructure where the villagers are the following:

- **The nodes and the miners**: They are the entities that validate the transactions and store the ledger (more on that later).
- They are **the users of the service** provided by the network. In this example, the service is the ability to use a decentralized means of payment (Villagecoin) to sell and purchase physical goods. It can be compared to Bitcoin.

So far, we have seen some quite interesting things. We already demonstrated the decentralization feature of the blockchain and how a database can be shared and track-recorded across a network without being altered.

 We have shown three important characteristics that define a blockchain: it is a shared, transparent, and distributed database.

Now comes the most important and hardest feature to understand: security.

The security factor

As stated before, each page of the book is designed with 10 lines. So, *what happens when we get to transaction number #10?* We surely need to go to the next page. However, before doing so, the villagers must validate the transactions and seal the page.

To keep the transactions secured, the villagers decide that each page must be removed from the book and put away on a special wall that will display each page once it is completed. This way, the villagers will be sure that the transactions (hence, the pages) displayed on the wall are true, valid, and correct.

In the blockchain world, the pages are the **blocks** that contain the transactions. We can compare the wall as the entire blockchain, where all of the validated pages are displayed (in other words, where the blocks are chained together). If one transaction is altered in a block, then all of the following transactions in the subsequent blocks become invalid.

Let's stick to the example to understand how it works.

Processing the blockchain

The wall that displays the valid pages will not let any villager put his/her page on it. After a page is completed with 10 transactions recorded, only one villager gets to put his/her page on it. To do so, all of the villagers will have to compete to find the result of a mathematical problem.

Here is the **delicate part** that makes a blockchain immutable and unalterable.

There is a section on the wall that has two small screens that will display some information every time a page is completed:

- On **Screen A**, a number is displayed that we will call *the reference number.*
- On **Screen B**, the date and time are displayed.

Under these two screens, there are two other screens where the villagers will input data:

- On **Screen C**, the villagers will input the 10 transactions of the completed page.
- On **Screen D**, the villagers will input a random number we will call *number X.*

Finally, a final screen displays a rule that must be respected when solving the mathematical problem, as shown in the following diagram:

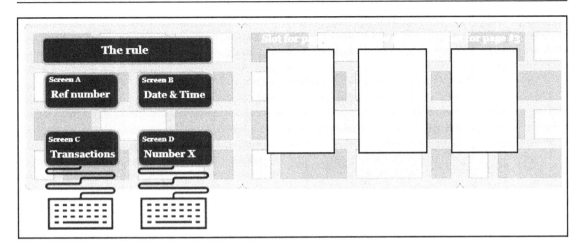

To keep this chapter's consistency and help you to understand everything, we will further define the rule, the reference number, and number X. Everything will make sense by the end of this chapter. For now, just move on with how pages are completed and displayed on the wall.

When page #1 is completed, all of the villagers gather before the wall to take notice of the information provided in the two first screens. In our example, we have the following:

- Screen A: Reference number: 0
- Screen B: Date and time: 2018/06/25, 03:25 PM

The rule given on the wall is as follows:

"The output number to be found when solving the mathematical problem must start with two leading zeros."

Do you remember that, for a page to be accepted on the wall, the villagers will have to solve a mathematical problem?

Well, this problem is set like this:

Screen A's reference number + Screen B's date and time + Screen C's transactions of the page + Screen D's random number input by the villager (number X) = an output number following the rule given by the wall (a number that starts will two leading zeros)

In this equation, we actually know four out of the five variables:

- Data from **Screen A** (the reference number) is given by the wall: **0**.
- Data from **Screen B** (the date and time) is given by the wall: **2018/06/25**, 03:25 PM.
- Data from **Screen C** (the transactions) are to be filled by the villagers. They are written on the pages of their books.
- Data from **Screen D** (the rule) is given by the wall: The output number to be found when solving the mathematical problem must start with two leading zeros

The equation can be pictured like this:

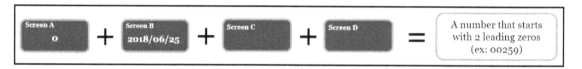

Now, the hard part for the villagers is to find the correct number to enter on **Screen D** for the equation to return a number that respects the rule of the wall: a number starting with two leading zeros.

To help you to visualize the mathematical problem, it can roughly be represented like this:

$$4 + 2 + 1 + number X < 10$$

For this equation, the answer would be easy because we know that we have to add the numbers together and *number X* to find an output lower than 10. Here, *number X* would be equal to 1 or 2:

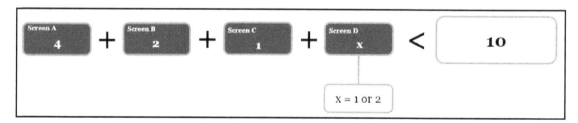

However, in Village Beta, no one knows the wall's algorithm. No one knows the logic of it and how the problem should be computed. They will have to try a lot of different *number X* solutions to find the correct output.

Breaking down blockchains

In this section, we shall try to break down the mathematical problem, *number X*, the reference number, the rule, and how they work together to allow recording transactions in a consensual and secured manner.

Let's summarize what we have so far:

- The page is what we call a **Block**.
- Date time provided on screen B is what we call the **timestamp** of the block.
- *Number X* is known as a **nonce**. It is the number that the nodes of the blockchain network (in our example, the villagers) try to find to reach the output number that respects the rule given by the wall.
- The process of finding *number X* is called **mining**.
- The rule given by the wall is called a **hash function**.
- We will see what the reference number is, in later sections.

The hash function

Before moving on with the mathematical problem, let's first focus on the rule given by the wall, the so-called hash function.

A hash function is a mathematical function that transforms any chain of characters or numbers into a fixed-length chain of characters. It turns data **into a digital fingerprint called a hash**. For example, if I enter `euclide` (7 characters) into the hash function called SHA-256, it will return the 64 characters hash:
`E0F4C627CD4D365EE9760BAA6A1CD35CA26CF7252F6EB25C0DC7B4C3E2718A20`.

 SHA stands for **Secure Hash Algorithm** and is a set of cryptographic hash functions designed by the US National Security Agency. SHA-256 means that it is a hash function producing a 256-bit-long output.

Now, if I input into the same SHA-256 hash function the entire Wikipedia's Bitcoin page description, it will return:
`D5752C643EC97DC0FF32AE74FF2F2079043A8AB0191C51AEFDE09EDE0C757EE6`.

It returns 64 characters—all of the time—whatever the length of the input is.

The hash function is deterministic: it is always the same output for the same input.

The following diagram depicts the process explained in this section:

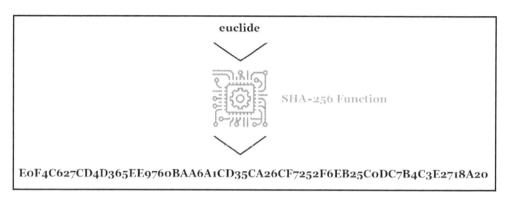

The principle behind a hash function is, when you know the output, it is very hard to find the input because the reverse action is not possible. That is, knowing the digital fingerprint of data does not reveal that specific data. You cannot guess that I entered `euclide` if I tell you that the output is `E0F4C627CD4D365EE9760BAA6A1CD35CA26CF7252F6EB25C0DC7B4C3E2718A20`. However, when knowing the input, it is very easy to find the correct output. Indeed, you can easily verify that `euclide` returns the hash `E0F4C627CD4D365EE9760BAA6A1CD35CA26CF7252F6EB25C0DC7B4C3E2718A20`, just by entering it into the SHA-256 hash function.

 You can try this yourself on your device. Try typing `euclide` on the following website: `https://passwordsgenerator.net/sha256-hash-generator`. You should find the same chain of characters as mine.

If we return to Village Beta, you might have understood where this is going:

- The reference number, 0
- + the timestamp of the page, 2018/06/25, 03:25 PM
- + the transactions (the data written in one page of the book)
- + the nonce (number X)
- = return the hash of page #1 (an output number following the rule: a number starting with two leading zeros)

The preceding equation can be pictured like this:

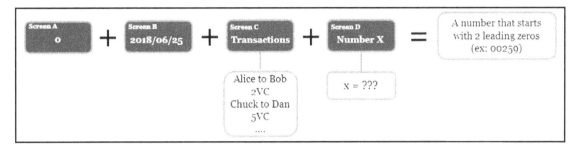

Consequently, to find the output number (a number starting with two leading zeros, or the hash of the page), every villager will have to try several inputs for *number X* for the equation to return a number respecting the rule.

It is as if I asked you: using the SHA-256 hash function, can you find an output number starting with two leading zeros? How many inputs will you try before finding a correct output?

You can also try this exercise on your device, using this website: `https://passwordsgenerator.net/sha256-hash-generator`.

The missing variable

Eventually, one villager, named Dan, finds an appropriate *number X*. He tells everybody else that the number **12345**, combined with the timestamp, the reference number, and the transactions return the output number, **0031993**. As regards the rule, this number is a valid output because it starts with two leading zeros.

Because it is very easy to find the output when you know the input, every other villager can verify that *number X*, 12345, is a correct data that return a valid hash, that is, for the mathematical problem to be solved.

The output **0031993** is what we call the **hash value of a block**. It is the seal needed for the page and its transactions to remain valid.

Once everyone has verified that 12345 is the correct *number X* (the nonce) that returns the output number 0031993 (the hash value) that respects the rule, Dan is allowed to display his first page on the wall, hence becoming the reference page:

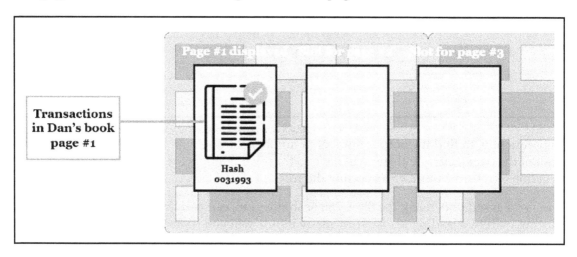

The incentives mechanism

Now, why should every villager try to find *number X* since somebody is going to find it anyway and tell everyone else? Why should a villager spend time and effort to have his/her page validated and displayed on the wall?

We introduce here the incentive mechanism, an economic payoff for the community to play fair. Because the pages should keep being sealed to keep the transactions accurate, the community should continuously work on solving the mathematical problem. In this manner, a reward is given to the villager who finds *number X*, that is, the first villager to find the correct hash of the page. In our example, Dan is rewarded with, say, 5 Villagecoin.

This incentive mechanism ensures that everyone keeps interested in working for the common good. More on that in Chapter 2, *A Technical Dive into Blockchain*.

Now that page #1 is displayed on the wall and secured, transactions continue to take place: *Chuck sends 5 Villagecoin to Alice, Dan sends 2 Villagecoin to Bob*, and so on.

When page #2 is completed with 10 transactions, the villagers repeat the entire process all over again.

The chain

So, what is the *reference number*? Remember that, on page #1, the reference number was 0?

For page #2, it will be 0031993. Exactly! The reference number of page #2 is the output number found for the previous page. In technical terms, we call it the **previous hash** or **the hash value of the previous block**. This allows the pages to be linked with one another, or to be chained to one another.

So, when page #2 is filled, the process repeats: every villager gathers at the wall, which displays new information on screens A and B:

- Screen A's reference number (hash of the previous page, page #1): 0031993
- Screen B's date and time (timestamp): 2018/07/03, 10:08 AM

The following diagram displays the new information on the wall:

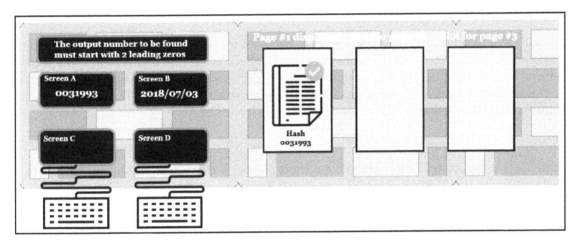

Then, the villagers input the transactions of page #2 in Screen C. Finally, everyone tries to find the correct *number X* (the nonce) on Screen D, which will return an output number starting with two leading zeros.

When an output number following the rule is found, *number X* is announced to everyone else who checks that *number X*, combined with 0031993, the timestamp, and the transactions, returns a number that starts with two leading zeros. If everyone agrees, we put the page on the wall and reward the villager who found the correct input with 5 Villagecoin.

And then the process repeats with page #3, page #4, and so on:

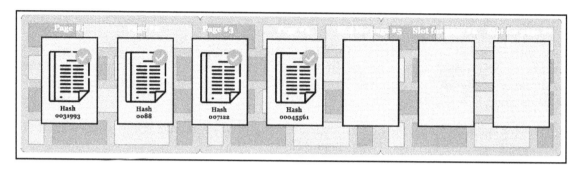

Let's evaluate how secured this system is. Let's assume that Chuck wants to modify a transaction on page #2. He wants to erase the 5 Villagecoin he sent to Alice during the completion of page #2, and change it to 1 Villagecoin.

What will happen?

He will have to solve again the mathematical problem for page #2 because he modified the transaction of page #2 (hence, the data of Screen C). Because of this slight change, the wall returns an entirely different output number, say 37882, which does not respect the rule anymore. Therefore, Chuck has to calculate the new *number X* on Screen D that would return a number starting with two leading zeros for page #2.

How is that a complication for Chuck?

Imagine that Chuck actually finds a new correct *number X* that returns an output number that starts with two leading zeros. Because hash functions are change-sensitive (a slight modification in the input returns a totally different output), even if Chuck finds a new correct input, the output will totally be different from the original. Say the new output number for page #2 is 00829 instead of the initial 0088. What will happen on page #3? The reference number (previous hash) will be different and so will be the output number of page #3. Furthermore, it is very likely that the new reference number of page #3 (00829 instead of 0088) combined with the rest of the data on the other screens will return a number that does not start with two leading zeros, hence making the page (and the transactions with it) invalid. In this fashion, Chuck will also have to compute again *number X* of page #3, then of page #4 and #5 and every page validated afterward.

This is how security is achieved in a blockchain, by sealing and chaining the blocks containing the transactions.

The more pages (blocks) are put on the wall (validated), the more secure and unalterable are the transactions. Because it would take a tremendous amount of time and computing power to re-calculate every *number X* (nonce) of every page (blocks) in order to find the correct output numbers that start with two leading zeros (hashes), the wall (the blockchain) is the best technology for storing and securing the transactions of the villagers (nodes and users).

Summary

Throughout this chapter, we got a foothold in blockchain by introducing the main economic aspects and challenges, discovering, with the simplest example, what this technology is about and how it works. The Villagecoin case is a realistic representation of Bitcoin, the first blockchain application ever and the most famous one. It is an imaginary situation that illustrates how decentralization and distributed ledgers enhance cooperation between individuals that do not trust each other, allowing them to exchange value without any confiding intermediary. Hopefully, we also demonstrated, in the most comprehensible way, what are hashes and nonces, which enable the blocks to be chained together, bringing security in a decentralized infrastructure, at least in those based on this mechanism. But more on that later.

In the next chapter, we will discover how cryptography, consensus mechanisms, and peer-to-peer networks can achieve mass coordination in a trustless environment. In other words, we are going to explore, in a technical sense, the main features and components of a blockchain.

2
A Technical Dive into Blockchain

Because digital ubiquity raises more and more concern for decision-makers to be able to thrive and adapt their businesses to emerging trends and shifts in consumption habits, new technologies have to be well apprehended. Blockchain, as a matter of fact, is a new enabler that must be understood properly when considering an innovation strategy for your company.

First of all, there are different types of blockchain but the general idea behind them is the same. Mainly, they aim to solve trust issues between strangers willing to exchange value in the digital world. Secondly, even though we can distinguish several kinds of blockchain such as public or semi-private infrastructures (more on that in `Chapter 9`, *Infrastructures and Cloud-Based Solutions*), they all integrate similar components.

Throughout this chapter, we will discover how the network empowers the blockchain, how hashes allow transactions and information to be secured, how digital identities are managed, and how game theory and economics enable responsible behavior. We will also have a look at the original problem that blockchain was the answer to and eventually discover what kind of consensus protocol can be implemented to achieve mass coordination within the network. Each component will be described as a sole instrument but we shall adopt a holistic view when we combine them all together. Therefore, one section can appear unclear when read separately but, by the end of this chapter, you should appreciate the functioning of the whole infrastructure and the role of each feature that come together to form a blockchain.

In this chapter, we will cover the following topics:

- Enliven the blockchain with the network
- Cryptography and hash functions
- The data structure
- Managing digital identities
- The Byzantine Generals Problem
- The incentive mechanism
- Achieving consensus

No network, no blockchain

A blockchain's most important component is the network—which is the community empowering it. The role of the community is to ensure that the truth is correctly recorded in the shared database.

The following diagram is an overview of a blockchain layer:

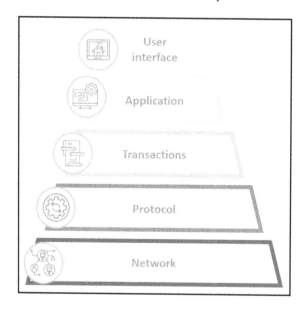

To understand this in a better way, let's look at a metaphorical example.

Truth in the network

Imagine a US Open final is happening next weekend between Roger Federer and Rafael Nadal. Being a big fan of Roger Federer and being sure he will win the game, Alice bets $10 on the betting website Betwin. On the other hand, Bob, who is an experienced gambler, thinks that Rafael Nadal will win. Bob decides to place a $10 bet on the Betwin platform on Rafael Nadal's victory.

Because Betwin is a private company, its objective is to maximize its profit. To do so, the company could tell Alice that Rafael Nadal won the game and tell Bob that Roger Federer won the game. In this manner, Betwin could hold both bets without having to pay either Alice or Bob.

Why is this method preposterous for Betwin?

The evident explanation is that Alice and Bob will not only believe Betwin to know the result of the game. They will check press releases, have a look at internet news, or ask their friends. And unless Betwin can make the press, the internet news, and Alice and Bob's friends announce the result that suits them best, their method will not work. In short, Alice and Bob do not trust only one third party, but instead, rely on the network to know the truth. And until there is no proof that Betwin controls the network, Alice and Bob will always know the truth.

 In a blockchain, the information that the majority of the community agrees on as being true is recorded on the database that is shared among all members.

The information added to the database is also checked with previous information already registered. In our example, Novak Djokovic cannot win the US Open final because there is information in the database stating that he already lost the previous round.

Let's move on to look at the various key roles within a blockchain network.

Participants in the network

Once again, the network is a very important feature in a blockchain—it has to be decentralized enough to be sure that the majority is not controlled by a single entity. It has to be heterogeneous enough so that the truth is represented by the majority. To achieve decentralization and heterogeneity, data must be distributed across the community. It should be distributed to anyone who wants to participate with no condition or barriers, forming a network of computers interacting with each other.

The network layer of a blockchain is also known as a peer-to-peer network.

In a centralized system, devices such as phones or computers access information to a central server that is owned by one entity. In a decentralized system supported by a peer-to-peer network, all of the devices, including the servers, interact and communicate with each other independently. These devices are called **nodes**. Each node can share information with any other node, without relying on a central server. Examples of such networks are the infamous file-sharing applications, BitTorrent, uTorrent and eMule, enabling users to download from and share data. When you are a participant of a peer-to-peer network, you act both as a provider and a consumer of files retrieved through other nodes. These are the kind of networks that enable decentralization within a blockchain. No entity is proprietary of the data nor has the exclusive right to read or modify the database.

The story of Napster is a revealing example of the weaknesses showed in a centralized system, especially in terms of control. Napster was a music file-sharing application that was shut down in 2001 after a long legal action undertook by record companies complaining about a violation of copyrights. Although Napster worked upon a peer-to-peer network, it centrally maintained a directory of all users and files. This configuration allowed the US district court to cease Napster's activity once the injunction was issued. The seizure would probably not have happened if the application relied on a true decentralized peer-to-peer network where the directories were stored by each node.

In a blockchain, there are several roles given to the participants of the network:

- **The users**: They utilize the application running on top of the blockchain. They do not own any data from that blockchain; they solely use the service.
- **The nodes**: These computers store the database on their memory and make it available for anyone to see the history of transactions or information.
- **The miners**: These computers run the software enabling the validation of blocks and transactions.

In certain blockchains, such as the one underpinning Bitcoin, anybody can become a miner, a node, or just a user. These kinds of blockchains are called public (or permissionless) as opposed to private (or permissioned) blockchains in which the roles are predefined for every participant. We will explore these differences further in the next chapters.

We will not technically describe how these nodes are connected but we will remember that, in a distributed system (in the end, that is what a blockchain is), the computers talk to each other to exchange information efficiently. Geolocation and power of the computers are variables that are taken into consideration when making the computers talk to each other.

Each node (and each miner) holds an identical copy of the blockchain. New miners and nodes download the entire history to the peers they are connected to if they want to be part of that network. The size of a blockchain can be pretty memory-consuming: at the time of writing this book, if you want to become a node of the Bitcoin blockchain, you must download a 223 GB file.

The responsibility of the miner is to do the following:

- Construct a new block with new transactions.
- Find the correct answer to the mathematical problem (the nonce) to validate the block.
- Spread it across the network for everyone to see and check.

For the blockchain to evolve, transactions need to occur continuously and get compiled in blocks by the miners who calculate the resulting hash before adding the block to the chain.

But how do the miners ensure that the suggested block does not include fake transactions? And how do they add it to the chain?

Cryptography

We talked about cryptography and hash functions in the first chapter where we defined what it was:

It is a mathematical function where, knowing the output, it is almost impossible to find the correct input. But knowing the input of the function, it is very easy to find the correct output. This is made possible because a hash function always returns the same output for the same input.

A hash is a result of a mathematical function that is a transformation applied to an input that generates an output. $Y = f(x)$ is a mathematical function where x is the input and Y is the output.

In mathematical terms, we have the following:

"Knowing Y, it is almost impossible to find x. But knowing x, it is very easy to find Y."

The hash function is essential to make information and transactions secured along the blockchain.

There are basic properties around a hash function that we have seen in `Chapter 1`, *Basics of Blockchains and the Illustration of Village Beta*:

- It is deterministic, meaning that it is always the same output for the same input.
- It has a defined range, meaning that any size of input can be injected in the function but it will always be the same length output. In other words, no matter the length of the input, the function will always return a fixed number of characters (in `Chapter 1`, *Basics of Blockchains and the Illustration of Village Beta*, the output length was 64 characters all the time because we were using the hash function, SHA-256).

But these properties are not enough to secure a transaction or a piece of information. There are other cryptographic properties surrounding hash functions used in a blockchain:

- It is **change-sensitive**, meaning that if one character of the input is modified, the output will totally be different.
- It is **non-invertible**, meaning that it should not be possible to determine efficiently the input of a given output, just like a padlock is not supposed to be deciphered.
- It is **collision-resistant**. A collision happens in a hash function when two different inputs generate the same output. Since inputs can have any length but outputs are fixed-length, obviously, there will be collisions. In other words, there is a finite number of possible outputs for an infinite number of inputs. Collision resistance means that finding two different inputs for the same output should not be possible using smart algorithms or strategy but only by trying every possibility. This is what we call **brute-force**.

What you have to remember for this section is that the hash value of an input can be used as the reference of that input. The hash value is the digital fingerprint of the input data, which can be a document, a transaction, or any kind of information. We can inject any file into the hash function and use the hash value to refer to it, hence uniquely identifying the document, the transaction, or the information.

Understanding the data structure

A blockchain can also be defined as a sequence of blocks containing data that are chained together. There are two types of data:

- Transactions
- Block information (also called metadata)

The transaction section is built by gathering all of the transactions that happened in a certain period of time and gathered in the block. If I send you one Bitcoin, this transaction will be part of the transaction section. Three fields are consistently active:

- The recipient
- The sender
- The amount

When I send you one Bitcoin using the Bitcoin blockchain, the transaction is composed as follows:

- The recipient is your account (your Bitcoin address).
- The sender is my account (my Bitcoin address).
- The amount is 1 Bitcoin.

 An example of a Bitcoin address is
3QSuhbsJUZJRgYX965CwMHgsdaU8KuTg4H.

Once all of the transactions are filled in the block, the block is hashed with the appropriate function (that is, the mining process occurs), which will return the **hash value of this block**, hence, of all transactions contained in the block. If one transaction of this block is modified afterward, the hash will change dramatically (the change-sensitive property) and the block would not be secured anymore.

Note that, depending on the blockchain, the validation span and the number of transactions of the block vary. For Bitcoin, one block is validated approximately every 10 minutes and contains several transactions fluctuating around 1,500 as of June 2019. This period is defined regarding the size limit of a block, that is, the number of transactions it can handle in one block. It is rather the size of the transactions that matter than the volume. That is why Bitcoin has an average block limit of 1,500 transactions—because it can sometimes handle more transactions and sometimes fewer. Transactions can become more complex if there are several senders or several recipients in one transaction. To put it in perspective, the Bitcoin blockchain handles 1 MB blocks, whereas the Bitcoin Cash blockchain handles 8 MB blocks.

 Bitcoin Cash was created in August 2017 by a section of the Bitcoin community to overcome Bitcoin's scalability issues through the extension of block size. Just like Bitcoin, it is a cryptocurrency and a blockchain.

Let's now have a look at the block information part, also called metadata. These pieces of information refer to the block itself and not to the transactions. If we think back to the example of `Chapter 1`, *Basics of Blockchains and the Illustration of Village Beta*, they refer to the following:

- The previous hash
- The timestamp
- The nonce
- The hash

The previous hash is the reference number found when validating the previous block. For the first block of a blockchain, it is 0 or any value that the network agrees on. Remember that hashes are what allow blocks to be chained together, hence making the whole chain tamper-proof. To do so, every block contains the hash of the previous block.

The timestamp is the time and date when the block is validated by the network.

The nonce is the variable to find when solving the mathematical problem to validate a block. When the miners are receiving new transactions, they run a complex mathematical problem to find the appropriate nonce that returns a correct hash.

Once the hash is found, the transactions are validated and the block is stored in the database.

In conclusion, a block is a container of all of the transactions that happened over a defined timespan that are hashed to return a digital fingerprint of all of these transactions. The following diagram is the mining process followed by the miners of the network:

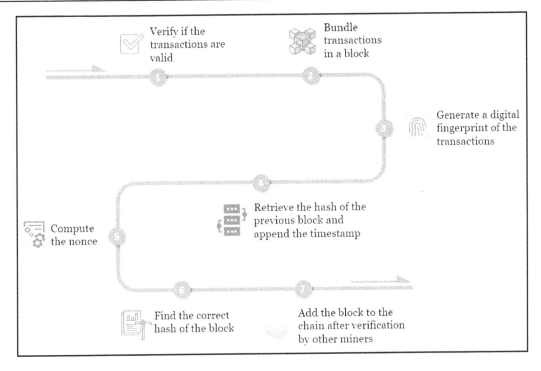

When building a block, the miners trigger a mining process using the hash of the previous block, the hash of all of the transactions, and the timestamp. The mining process ends when one of the miners finds the correct nonce that returns a valid hash (usually a number starting with a predefined number of zeros), which is tied to the block and will serve as the previous hash for the next block.

Creating identities

Most of the time, to use a service online, you must create an account with the organization that provides the service. If you want to use a social media application or create a bank account, you need to provide information on yourself for the organization to grant you access. This is the centralized model: identities are stored and managed on one central organization's servers. This is totally incompatible with the concept of blockchain that promotes decentralization to achieve mass-coordination without a central entity.

So, how do we create identities that are not controlled by any third party in that kind of ecosystem?

Securing identities using blockchain

In a blockchain, the person who sends the digital value and the person who receives it must be accurately determined.

Cryptography allows us to achieve just that, thanks to asymmetric encryption. Both asymmetric and symmetric methods basically achieve security through cryptography when sending a message or funds to someone, as well as being used to manage identities in a decentralized manner. Before explaining what asymmetric encryption is, which is used in most blockchains, we should explain what symmetric encryption is.

With the symmetric method, everyone has only one key to encrypt or decrypt a specific message. If I want to send you the message *Hello*, I will follow this process:

- I encrypt the message *Hello* that becomes, say, *Jrmmp*.
- I send you my encrypted key.
- You decrypt the message using my key.

The key is generated through an algorithm that allows someone who possesses the key to encrypt and decrypt the message.

But there is one important risk that exists using this encryption method. Since you need to send the recipient your key to allow him/her to read your messages (the process is called the handshake), a malicious person could intercept the key and use it afterward to decrypt your messages.

The asymmetric encryption, on the other hand, overcomes this problem. With this method, instead of one key, there are two keys, a public and a private key. The public key is communicated to anybody who wants to send you messages or digital value. The private key, on the contrary, is known by you and only you. It should never be disclosed to anyone else.

If I want to send you the message *Hello*, we would follow this process:

1. I retrieve your public key.
2. I encrypt the message *Hello* using your public key and send it to you.
3. You decrypt the message using your private key.

If a hacker intercepts the encrypted message I sent you, he/she won't be able to decrypt it because he/she doesn't possess the private key, which is the only key allowing the decryption of the message. In short, the public key is used to encrypt a message, and the private key to decrypt it.

There are two principles to remember with the asymmetric encryption's key pair—private key/public key; and they are the same as we've seen with the hash function:

- One private key when hashed always gives the same public key.
- Knowing the public key, it is impossible to find the private key (except with brute-force: by trying a lot of private keys).

 Brute-forcing a one-character password is relatively simple—64 combinations (a,b...A, B...1, 2...). But when it comes to the Bitcoin blockchain, whose private keys are 51 characters long, the probability reaches 64^51 possibilities. It would take years to brute-force a private key on the Bitcoin blockchain.

This asymmetric encryption allows you to digitally sign any kind of information, message or transaction. Otherwise, how would you prove in the digital world that you are the author of a specific message or the owner of a specific account?

Encryption with the private key is used to prove authenticity. If you encrypt your message with your own private key, then anyone can decrypt it with your public key, which proves that you originated the message since it could only have been encrypted with your private key.

In this scenario, your public key is your digital identity since it identifies statements and information made by you in the digital world. The private key is a kind of password to prove that you own your public key, that is, your digital identity.

This is how we achieve decentralized identity management. Usually, the public key refers to the address of the account. Also, you don't have to link your real identity with your digital identity. Just by generating a new key pair, you would end up with a new digital identity. Keep in mind that this does not provide you with full anonymity because some information or statements sent with your digital identity may tie you with your real identity. That is why the Bitcoin blockchain is not entirely anonymous but rather pseudonymous.

The Byzantine Generals Problem

In the following chapters, we will start addressing more business-oriented topics. Until then, I should provide you with some context on the whys and wherefores of blockchain and go back to where it all started, with the Byzantine Generals Problem.

The Byzantine Generals Problem is a real-life analogy for computer science that was expressed and partly answered in 1982 by Leslie Lamport, a famous American scientist and Turing Award winner, who raised the following question: *how can you achieve a consensus in the presence of traitors or faults?* Translated to the computer science world, this means: *how can you achieve consensus in a distributed system where some computers may be malfunctioning or give conflicting information?* This is how the issue came to be illustrated and known as the Byzantine Generals Problem.

The following diagram is an illustration of the Byzantine Generals Problem:

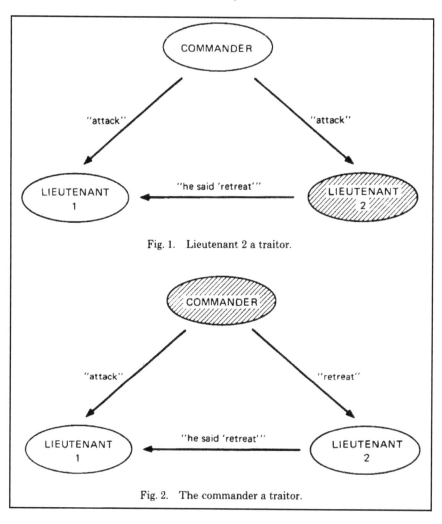

Fig. 1.   Lieutenant 2 a traitor.

Fig. 2.   The commander a traitor.

Source: L.Lamport, R.Shostak and M.Pease, The Byzantine Generals problem, ACM Transactions on Programming Languages and Systems, Vol. 4, No. 3, July 1982

Explanation—multiple byzantine generals surrounding a city must coordinate their attack to take the city. To coordinate themselves, they use messengers to indicate to each other which decision they took: attack or retreat. Since this situation happens under war circumstances, some generals could be traitors and some messengers could be captured or die trying to send the news.

If we draw a comparison with blockchain, the generals are the miners and the messengers are the communication links between them. Several researchers have concluded that the generals can't agree on a strategy if one third or more are traitors.

So how does blockchain solve it?

One instrument was introduced into the blockchain to make consensus work: **incentives**. A blockchain usually includes incentives for the miners who validate the transactions. In `Chapter 1`, *Basics of Blockchains and the Illustration of Village Beta,* the villager who validated the transactions was rewarded with 5 Villagecoin.

In a blockchain, this is how a consensus is reached:

1. All of the miners start constructing their local block.
2. A random miner solves the mathematical problem of the block.
3. The random miner sends his/her block to the other miners.
4. The other miners receive the block of the random miner.
5. The other miners check that the result found by the random miner is correct and that the previous hash points to the previous block's hash.
6. If it is valid, they cancel the block they were building and add to the copy of their blockchain the new block sent by the random miner.
7. The random miner is rewarded with an incentive.
8. Then, the process repeats.

If a dishonest miner solved the mathematical problem and incorporated an invalid transaction in its block, the other miners would reject it because it contains an invalid transaction (the hash would totally be different). This miner would have to discard his/her block and, therefore, will not be able to receive any incentive. Let's look at how incentives work in more detail.

Offering incentives

Basically, incentives ensure that miners continue working for the network responsibly (in other words, consensually validate correct transactions). The work provided by the miners is rewarded by the cryptocurrency underlying the blockchain. By implementing rewards, people are encouraged to join the community and become miners, who, as a result, contribute to broadening the network. And the more miners there are, the larger the network and the more secured are the transactions because the less chance there is for the blockchain to be controlled by one party or individual.

Note that the rewards are usually decreasing exponentially over time because a blockchain often starts with few miners before enjoying a network effect and attracting more miners. Joining a blockchain early as a miner ensures you to gain more cryptocurrency even though it is not worth much at the beginning. But as more miners are joining the network and as more users are using the service, the cryptocurrency itself starts gaining consideration, hence, value. In this manner, rewards for miners usually decline over time following a predefined algorithm as more members join the network. For Bitcoin, for example, the original block reward was 50 Bitcoin, planned to halve every 210,000 blocks. As of June 2019, the block rewards are 12.5 BTC and total supply is set to 21 million BTC, the last unit of which should be allocated in 2140. What is important to remember as a decision-maker is that incentivization is an important component of a blockchain because it answers the following question: what are the interests for a miner to continue to validate the transactions happening in the network? Put differently, what is the motivation of the validators to keep ensuring the truth within the registry?

Understanding the consensus protocol mechanism

As stated before, for the miners to validate a block and, hence, the transactions, they have to solve a mathematical problem. To solve it, there is a need for a specific resource. In Bitcoin, the resource is computing power. The more computing power a miner has, the faster he/she can solve the mathematical problem, therefore the faster he/she completes a block and the more likely he/she will receive Bitcoins as a reward. This mining process is called proof-of-work and is inherent to Bitcoin. It is a protocol that all of the miners of the Bitcoin blockchain should follow to demonstrate that they have done an appropriate work for validating the transactions. This ensures a selection process in which every miner uses computational power to find the correct nonce that will return a hash starting with a predefined number of zeros. Of course, not all miners have the same computing power, so it is not fairly random.

The computing power of a machine is measured by the number of guesses per second.

The most powerful miners will have more chances to solve the problem compared to sole computers with less computing power. However, even if one owns 10% of the computing power of the entire network and the 90% remaining are provided by thousands of other miners, one will still have a 1 in 10 chance of finding the correct answer. This is how randomness ensures that no one can control the validation of the blocks and, hence, the blockchain. This also means that if one miner, or one organization of miners, came to control 51% or more of the computing power of the network, they would be the first to solve the problem in 51% of the cases. In other words, they would be able, in 51% of the cases, to validate or modify the transactions at their will.

There is one important issue behind the proof-of-work protocol that, as a decision-maker, you should be aware of—it is a very energy-consuming process that leverages questions on its sustainability. Since it takes a tremendous amount of computing power to find the proper hash of the block and since there are a lot of miners in the network, the consumption of electricity for validating the transactions on the Bitcoin blockchain has become a worldwide concern to the point that it has exceeded the consumption of electricity of Switzerland (`https://www.bbc.com/news/technology-48853230`). The following diagram shows Bitcoin's energy consumption as of June 2019:

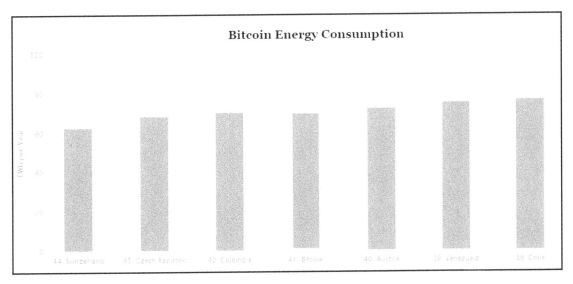

Source: `https://digiconomist.net`

Of course, other protocols can replace the energy-consuming proof-of-work. One of the most well known is proof-of-stake, which is being implemented in the Ethereum blockchain. But more on that in the next chapter, Chapter 3, *Ethereum and Smart Contracts*.

Summary

All in all, a blockchain is the combination of several instruments that come together to provide an infrastructure to exchange digital value and assert the truth without the need of a central entity.

As discussed throughout this chapter, a blockchain is composed of a network of users, nodes, and miners that respectively send/receive, store, and validate transactions. Cryptography (and more specifically hash functions) is used in this configuration to create an output (a hash) that refers to any kind of digital information, for example, to refer to a batch of transactions. Blocks cluster these transactions and include metadata associated with the block itself such as the previous hash, the timestamp, and the nonce. Public and private keys provide a way to efficiently manage identities in the digital world and more specifically in the network. In a blockchain, there is also an incentive mechanism where the underlying cryptocurrency is used as a reward to motivate miners to work for the common good and keep ensuring the truth across the blockchain. Finally, a consensus protocol comes in to enable the miners to validate the transactions continuously and properly.

At this point, you hopefully understand how a blockchain works and what intrinsic principles it combines to ensure security, transparency, and immutability. So far, we have covered the most important characteristics. The better you appreciate them, the easier it will be for you to grasp the main social and economic challenges surrounding blockchain and eventually help you to identify the relevance of a blockchain for a specific use case.

In the next chapter, we will learn about Ethereum and smart contracts.

3
Ethereum and Smart Contracts

Ethereum is one of the most prominent projects in the blockchain ecosystem. It was officially launched in July 2015 in order to overcome some of Bitcoin's major limitation. A new programming language was created to enable the development of much more sophisticated operations than those used in Bitcoin. The goal of Ethereum is to allow the creation of **decentralized applications (dApps)** upon its infrastructure with the help of a unit of account called Ether, facilitating the developer's job by solely focusing on the service rather than the protocol. Ethereum was the first platform to introduce new concepts such as smart contracts and dApps, which brought to blockchain technology more user-friendliness and, of course, more applications for the end users than a sole cryptocurrency such as Bitcoin. One could now develop from scratch a new application based on Ethereum's easy and already-running infrastructure. The development of many dApps followed the launch, which contributed to a wide democratization of the blockchain technology. Today, Ethereum supports more than 1,800 dApps, which makes it the largest public blockchain platform.

This chapter will give you an overview of the differences and similarities between Bitcoin and Ethereum. Analyzing Ethereum in relation to Bitcoin is a good starting point to grasp the important advancements Ethereum brought to the blockchain ecosystem. The chapter will then give an explanation of the **Ethereum Virtual Machine** (**EVM**), a *world computer* enabling the creation of dApps. We will also look at smart contracts and the concept of gas, which always come along together. Finally, we will explain the differences between the consensus algorithm used in Bitcoin and the one that Ethereum tries to implement.

This chapter will address the following topics:

- Bitcoin versus Ethereum
- The EVM
- Comparing proof-of-work and proof-of-stake
- Real-world applications

Which is better, Bitcoin or Ethereum?

In the previous chapters, we learned all about Bitcoin—a cryptocurrency offering an alternative to traditional centralized payment systems based on a blockchain, which is a decentralized, shared, transparent, and secured database storing every transaction occurring on the network. Because Bitcoin is increasingly being used as a means of payment in retail and online stores, it is now seen as an asset class.

Just like any other asset class or investment product, Bitcoin suffers from the evolution of the financial markets while its supporters regard it for what it really is—a digital currency allowing almost instantaneous, secured, and cheap financial transactions between individuals across the globe.

In these terms, Ethereum is almost the same:

- It is a cryptocurrency (called Ether) enabling people to make financial transactions.
- It is backed by a blockchain that is also relying on the proof-of-work consensus protocol.

 Ethereum is currently moving toward a proof-of-stake consensus protocol throughout several updates and will reach its final version between 2020 and 2021. But more on that in the upcoming sections.

Since the creation of Bitcoin in 2009, there has not been any major advancement in the ecosystem. This was until the creation of Ethereum, which took blockchain and cryptocurrencies to the next level. What differentiates Ethereum from Bitcoin is the applications running on its blockchain. While the sole application running on Bitcoin's blockchain is Bitcoin, the so-called cryptocurrency, the Ethereum blockchain, on the other hand, can do much more. There are an unbelievable number of applications running on it, including the cryptocurrency Ether, which is used as a means of payment and which is very similar to Bitcoin.

Ethereum is often defined as a *world computer* or *platform* that can be used by anyone to create or operate dApps based on smart contracts. You can think of it as the Apple App Store or Google Play Store, in which you can buy and use different applications. However, Ethereum is decentralized, thus not owned by anyone, unlike Apple or Google, which centralize data and payments on their servers.

Another difference with Bitcoin is that while Bitcoin's inventor, **Satoshi Nakamoto**, remains unknown until now, Ethereum's founder is very popular in the ecosystem. His name is **Vitalik Buterin**, and he is a Russian-born Canadian programmer who came up with Ethereum's proposition in 2013. Just like any other blockchain, Ethereum relies on people powering the network to run a software on their computer. For Bitcoin, this software is BitcoinCore. For Ethereum, it is called the EVM.

The EVM

The EVM is like Windows or macOS, an operating system reading and understanding programs written in Ethereum's specific language: Solidity. It is a Turing-complete software that enables anyone to run any program, making the process of creating blockchain-based applications much easier and more efficient than ever before.

That is why there are thousands of different applications running on Ethereum's blockchain, because you do not have to write an entirely new language to be able to build an application.

 A Turing-complete machine is a concept of a machine that can calculate anything if it has unlimited memory available. Actual computers have to operate on limited memory, therefore they cannot be called Turing-complete. The Ethereum blockchain, on the other hand, is a distributed Turing-complete program.

Say you want to create a new coin that would be used only in a certain kind of shops. With the EVM, you do not have to build a blockchain from scratch but rather write a specific program in it and pay with Ethereum's native cryptocurrency, Ether, to spread it across the network and allow anyone to use it. We call this type of program a smart contract.

Understanding smart contracts

To understand smart contracts, let's take a real application that was created by Axa, a French leading insurance group. In September 2017, Axa launched an application called **fizzy**, a cancellation insurance product that automatically reimburses clients subjected to delayed flights.

Based on Ethereum, fizzy's smart contract stores the insurance subscribed by policyholders in a secure manner. It then connects to global air traffic databases to check whether a flight has been delayed and automatically triggers the compensation according to these parameters. This product offers a frictionless experience to the user and has been a great success for Axa. The following is a screenshot of Axa's **fizzy** landing page:

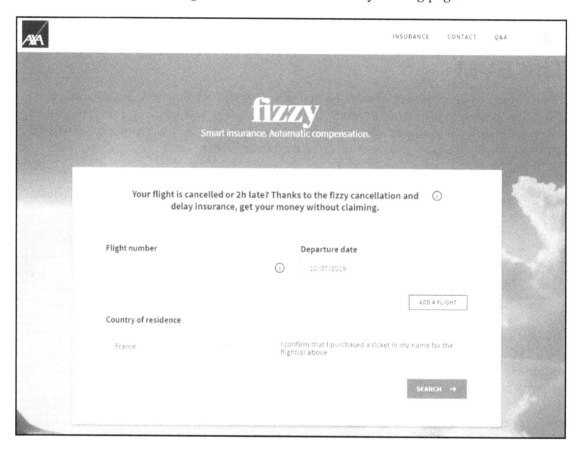

In short, a smart contract is a code written on the blockchain that applies the following rule:

IF [*condition*] THEN [*output*]

For fizzy, it is rewritten as the following:

IF [*flight number AF-03 is late more than 2 hours*] THEN [*reimburse purchase to travelers*]

Ethereum considers smart contracts and human users as the same. Both can send and receive Ether. However, smart contracts can execute certain actions when predefined conditions written in the contract are met.

Let's take another simple but self-evident example.

Consider two people betting on who's going to win the Rugby World Cup in 2019. Both agree to the condition that the loser gives $50 to the winner.

How do we ensure that the loser will indeed pay the winner?

- Either both players trust each other because they have been friends for a long time or get along very well.
- If they do not know each other, they have the possibility to sign a legal agreement. If there is a dispute on the payment, they could refer to the legal agreement, but the fees and time to get the situation fixed would be really high and harrowing for each other.
- Another possibility would be for them to give $50 each to a common trusted friend who would take care of the prize and would give it to the winner. But what if the so-called trusted friend runs away with the money?

I think it's easy to see that every option comes with its own downsides. Ethereum, however, can solve this problem using the smart contract feature.

The smart contract is like the trusted friend except it's in code. It will ensure that the winner genuinely receives the prize on the day we know the 2019 World Cup winning team.

A smart contract, once written, cannot be edited or altered. Once shared across the network, the conditions listed in the smart contract will be executed no matter what, thereby becoming unalterable.

And because developers can write unreasonable code or statements that have infinite loops causing a node to get stuck in the execution of a smart contract, Ethereum's developers came up with a way out. They invented the gas.

Gas

Gas is the cost of electricity, storage, and computation power spent by the miners to process a smart contract. Gas is a tiny portion of Ether.

> *"Because all these different actors [the nodes] are providing their resources to run the platform, you need to pay them for providing their resources."*

- Ethereum's co-founder Joseph Lubin

When executing a smart contract, a maximum level of gas is defined by the developer, ensuring that when it is reached, the smart contract stops being executed, preventing the nodes from running a poorly coded smart contract.

Antonio Madeira, Head of Advertising at `cryptocompare.com`, has a nice explanation:

> *"The more complex the commands you wish to execute, the more gas (and Ether) you have to pay. For example, if A wants to send B, 1 Ether unit—there would be a total cost of 1.00001 Ether to be paid by A. However if A wanted to form a contract with B depending on the future price of Ether, there would be more lines of code executable and more of an onus or energy consumption placed on the distributed Ethereum network—and therefore A would have to pay more than the 1 Gas done in the transaction."*

Even though dApps have many advantages, their relying smart contract can sometimes incorporate flaws. Do not forget that their code is written by humans!

Since a smart contract is immutable, the only way to correct the code is to reach a network consensus to agree to rewrite the code.

The reason why Ether is not the currency used to process smart contract is that Ether is too sensitive to market value. By linking gas to Ether and fixing the gas price to specific actions, the Ethereum community has ensured that the network will always perform the execution of smart contracts regardless of Ether's price.

Identity management in the Ethereum blockchain is achieved with two types of accounts:

- **Externally owned accounts:** These accounts are held by users to transfer Ether. Just like in the Bitcoin blockchain, they have an associated public key that acts as an address and also an associated private key that provide access to the account.
- **Contract accounts or smart contracts:** They can store Ether but they can also store code. These accounts have also a public key address to send Ether to but, because they are not supposed to be owned by anyone, they do not possess any private key.

So far, we've seen the main differences with Bitcoin and learned about the EVM, which serves as an operating system for the network to execute smart contracts, these programs being written by developers to carry out certain actions when specific conditions are met. We have seen how smart contracts are processed and run thanks to gas, a small fraction of Ether that plays the role of both incentive and fees.

Let's now dive into Ethereum's consensus protocol, real-world applications, and Ethereum's oncoming challenges.

Comparing proof-of-work and proof-of-stake

Ethereum currently relies on the same consensus protocol as Bitcoin: proof-of-work. In order for the blocks and transactions to be validated, the miners of the network have to solve a mathematical problem, which, as of April 19, 2019, takes approximately 13 seconds.

When the result (hash) is found, it is spread to the network, which checks it and stores the blocks containing the transactions in the ledger. Then another mathematical problem rises to validate a new block and so on.

This consensus protocol proof-of-work has several downsides:

- It is **harmful for the environment** because it requires an impressive amount of electricity for the computers to find the suitable hash that will validate the block.
- It is **expensive, non-inclusive, and reserved for experts** because the mining process requires good chips, material, and computational power to be able to run the hash's calculation.
- It is **resource-intensive** and makes Ethereum hard to scale when the network endures a peak load.

Ethereum was looking for another way of mining that could replace the proof-of-work consensus mechanism and its aforementioned downsides. The developer community has decided to move to the proof-of-stake consensus mechanism, where having powerful chips won't help you mine better or faster.

The Ethereum community is willing to let anybody, with any kind of computer, participate in the validation of the transactions, eliminating the non-inclusive competition underlying proof-of-work mining.

Since February 28, 2019, Ethereum has migrated to a new version of its network called **Constantinople**, which brought several evolutions needed to implement proof-of-stake. This evolution is part of a wider roadmap aiming to build a scalable and robust platform.

Four main phases make up this roadmap:

- **Frontier:** This was the earliest implementation of Ethereum, before it went live in 2015.
- **Homestead:** This was implemented in early 2016 in order to stabilize the network and increase its efficiency.
- **Metropolis:** This was launched in October 2017 with the update called **Byzantium** and will end at some point in 2020 after implementing three other updates (among which is Constantinople on February 28, 2019).
- **Serenity:** This is the proposed final state of Ethereum, integrating the proof-of-stake protocol and features to handle large numbers of transactions per second.

The proof-of-stake protocol does not require miners to compute a mathematical problem like the proof-of-work. Instead, it is a consensus protocol in which the validation of the blocks relies on an algorithm that chooses a user according to the number of Ether (or stakes) they possess.

Thus, the larger the amount of Ether a user owns, the more likely they are to be chosen to validate a new block. The incentive usually associated with the validation of a block is replaced by the gas associated with the block, which is the sum of all transactions' gas.

Real-world applications

Ethereum has proven its usefulness several times in the past few years through successful applications, and has already disrupted some business models. One of the most interesting ones is slock.it (`https://slock.it/`). This is an application founded by Stephan Tual and the Jentzsch brothers in 2015, aiming to create an infrastructure for a better sharing economy.

Using Ethereum's blockchain, slock.it is willing to link any kind of physical object to a smart contract to allow anybody to use the object. An example often used by the founders is the renting of a flat. With slock.it, you can link your door lock to a smart contract, enabling someone who wants to rent your flat to pay the price linked to the smart contract, which will automatically unlock the door. This setup eliminates a trusted third party that you would usually have to rely on to ensure the payment and the action related to the execution of this payment. In other words, it connects the door lock itself with the tenant securely and transparently without an intermediary.

If you are looking for more examples of dApps, you can have a look at *State of the DApps* (`https://www.stateofthedapps.com/`), which catalogs every dApps project.

Just remember that because dApps run on the blockchain, they benefit from all its properties:

- **Transparency**: The transactions happening on Ethereum's blockchain are visible to anyone.
- **Immutability**: Once the transactions are validated by the miners and shared across the network, they cannot be altered or modified.
- **Security**: Its decentralized setup eliminates a single point of failure and cryptography ensures that no hacking is possible.

Summary

In this chapter, we distinguished what features Ethereum offers compared to Bitcoin, which is a sole cryptocurrency. We showed how the EVM acts as a world computer, enabling the creation of dApps and smart contracts. We covered the concept of gas, which plays the role of fuel within the infrastructure in order for the code to be run. Eventually, we approached the main differences between proof-of-work and proof-of-stake as well as the ambitious roadmap followed by Ethereum.

In the next chapter, we will discover another important advancement that Ethereum has brought to the blockchain ecosystem, an advancement that made top news at the end of 2017 and that enabled any project to raise millions within minutes: initial coin offerings.

4

ICOs and Tokenized Fundraising Methods

The financial realm was hit in 2017 by two major phenomena caused by cryptocurrencies and blockchain. The first one was a bubble that Bitcoin and other digital currencies such as Ether and Ripple witnessed from June to December, the latter actually gaining a 450-fold increase in value in less than eight months. High volatility triggered terrible consequences on cryptocurrencies' credibility of being strong financial instruments and real digital assets. This led most financial analysts, banks, and hedge funds to consider them as sole speculative and significantly risky investments supported by intangible value and unreasonable behaviors from the crowd. Stuck into a vicious circle, the mass media started to headline cryptocurrencies and blockchain, amplifying the phenomenon and dazzling investors with high returns on this new financial product which, inevitably, led to a sharp downfall from Christmas 2017 to mid-2018.

The second phenomenon, which was much less covered by the mass media, can actually be explained as the catalyst for the first phenomenon. That is, **initial coin offerings** (**ICOs**) have been around since 2013, but it was only in 2017 that they started to gain consideration. As being a new fundraising method rewarding backers with a newly created cryptocurrency, ICOs enable any project to be crowdfunded in a matter of minutes. Only eight projects were financed through ICOs in the first quarter of 2017 for a total amount of $14 million. But then the fervor started. Over the next three months, 30 projects were successfully closed, reaching a total amount of almost $1 billion. By the end of the year, more than $5.4 billion was raised through ICOs, with 875 ventures launched. It was now the time for investors to pick the right project that would become the next Bitcoin, Ethereum, or Ripple. During this frenetic period (which eventually paced down in the second semester of 2018), the ecosystem looked like a giant casino where, fostered by an irrational environment, investors were eager to win big and project leaders to raise quick before the bustle slackened.

Now that the ecosystem has become more consistent with ICOs, we will be able to explain with the benefit of hindsight what they and the other derived fundraising methods (**security token offering (STO)**, **equity token offering (ETO)**, and **initial token offering (ITO)**) are. We will illustrate their utilization through examples, describe what type of tokens can be sold, and explain what advantages they bring in terms of fundraising. We will also find out why these methods have shown great success while lifting regulatory constraints and ethical questions.

This chapter addresses the following topics:

- What are ICOs?
- Illustration of an ICO: the case of Ethereum
- Utility tokens and security tokens
- What is so revolutionary about ICOs?

What are ICOs?

An ICO is somewhat like an **initial public offering (IPO)**. Basically, it is a fundraising tool that trades a new cryptocurrency in exchange for an already existing currency. Instead of listing a share on a designated stock exchange like in an IPO, the company issues newly created coins that they put up for sale at a given price.

Put simply, it is a project funded by liquid money (Bitcoin, Ethereum, or fiat currencies (https://www.investopedia.com/terms/f/fiatmoney.asp)) against a new cryptocoin created specifically for a project. These new coins are called tokens and are basically blockchain-based digital coupons that are tradable from peer to peer in an irreversible way. By purchasing these digital coupons, investors believe in the project's success and the added value coming with their resale.

Traditionally, start-ups and companies can raise money through several financial tools:

- Getting a bank loan
- Launching a crowdfunding campaign
- Selling shares of their capital to private investors
- Going public by selling shares of their capital to public investors (IPO)

With tokens and blockchain, they can now raise money by creating new digital blockchain-based tokens that they sell over a certain period of time in order to raise liquid money that will help them finance their project. Their underlying argument is that these tokens will gain value in time and are exchangeable against another cryptocurrency.

To understand an ICO, it is sometimes interesting to draw parallels with IPOs. Investors in an IPO automatically receive certain rights attached to the shares they acquire (dividend, vote, ownership, and so on) that partly contribute to the share's intrinsic value. In an ICO, the tokens issued and sold to the investors only come along with the promise of the project's success. No right to dividend nor right to vote is assigned to the tokens purchased during the ICO. It is a major downside that is often brandished as a counter argument by its detractors.

Moreover, regarding the newness of this financing method, ICOs are mainly unregulated in some jurisdictions. A lot of projects have failed these last few years and a lot of scams have been identified. Also, most of the project leaders raise money before even having developed the product. Thus, it is a highly risky investment. For a venture capitalist, it is comparable to investing millions in a seed-stage start-up. A thorough upstream research is required before investing in such projects.

Despite this, some ICOs have been quite successful and the sums raised astronomical. Actually, in 2017, ICO financing has exceeded venture capital fundraising and has become the number-one method to finance blockchain start-ups (`https://www.cbinsights.com/research/blockchain-vc-ico-funding/`).

Illustration of an ICO – the case of Ethereum

One of the first significant ICOs was made by the famous Ethereum (see `Chapter 3`, *Ethereum and Smart Contracts*). The founder, Vitalik Buterin, and his team issued between July 22, 2014, and September 2, 2014, about 60 million Ether (the new cryptocoin or token) in exchange for 31,500 Bitcoin, equivalent at the time to $18.4 million.

With this money, they could design and code the future Ethereum platform, which was launched on July 30, 2015. The founders motivated the investors that this platform would allow people to build decentralized applications upon it. Investors were seduced and paid in Bitcoin in exchange for Ether, the currency that would later be used as the *fuel* for building applications through the platform. Back then, with 1 Bitcoin, you could purchase about 1,900 Ether, which as of June 19, 2019, is valued at $509,200. Well worth the investment!

By crafting a predefined number of coins, project leaders make a promise that these tokens will enable the investors to buy a service or product in the future or trade them against another cryptocurrency.

What is incredible with Ethereum is that they both showcased the power of ICO fundraising and enabled people to do the same. Indeed, having a platform like Ethereum allowing developers to build an application without building a blockchain from scratch, a lot of projects have seen the light through the platform. One could create an application and sell the tokens for further development against Ether or Bitcoin. Since the launch of the Ethereum platform, the rise of ICOs has been exponential.

The most prominent demonstration of the potential of the Ethereum platform was the **decentralized autonomous organization** (**DAO**), whose ICO was launched in May 2016. The aim of this application built on the Ethereum blockchain was to create a decentralized venture capital fund with a voting system ruled by DAO token holders.

Anyone holding a DAO token could vote for a project to be financed or not. This totally new way of governing an organization seduced around 11,000 investors, who financed the project with upto $150 million worth of Ether. Unfortunately, on June 17, 2016, a malicious group of hackers managed to exploit a breach within the DAO's code and seized control of $3.6 million Ether out of the $11.5 million Ether collected by the DAO.

This failure made people aware of both the care that needs to be taken in coding such applications and the potential for projects and ideas to be financed through ICOs.

Utility tokens and security tokens

Although most of the tokens issued during an ICO are technically similar, their use can be separated into two categories:

- Utility tokens
- Security tokens

When Ethereum launched its sale of Ether, they promised that those tokens would be utilized as a means of payment for using the Ethereum platform to create an application. This underlines that Ether is a token that enables its owner to use the platform, thus the product. In this fashion, **Ether is a utility token**.

When the DAO launched its sale of the DAO token, they promised that those tokens would be utilized as a voting right for further-financed projects and as a profitable *share*. The tokens would indeed provide financial returns to the owner resulting from the DAO's profits. In this fashion, **the DAO token was a security token**.

The distinction between the two comes from the **US Security and Exchange Commission (US SEC)**, which regulates security tokens in the same way as shares of a company. If a project is declared to issue security tokens, the company has to comply with US SEC regulations, especially the Securities Act of 1933, in which several obligations and requirements have to be fulfilled to be able to raise funds from accredited, professional, or individual investors. To determine whether the token is a utility token or a security token, the US SEC uses an audit called the **Howey test**. It was created by the Supreme Court upon jurisprudence of a real case that happened to the Howey Company in 1946. The test is based on few criteria to determine whether a transaction represents an investment contract. In other words, if a transaction generates profit for the investors based on the effort of the company or project they invested in, then the transaction should be considered an investment contract and should abide by US SEC regulations.

In this fashion, deciding whether a token is a utility token or a security token is a rather subjective matter. Although some tokens are very obvious, such as DAO tokens or Ether, others can be pretty hard to judge. It is more related to a personal analysis according to the questions addressed:

- Is it a token that will be spent to use the product or service of the project?
- Is it a token that will provide only returns in a certain cryptocurrency?
- Is it a token that will be usable on another platform or to buy other products or services?
- Is it a token that will help users develop a specific privilege within the project ecosystem?

The US SEC, being a federal independent organism, is not against ICOs but against fraudulent manipulations regarding investment contracts, especially when it is new of a kind. The US SEC and equivalent institutions in other countries have focused their attention on ICOs, mostly because the legal frame is still mainly undefined. As it takes many legal resources and a consequent amount of money to comply with US SEC requirements, lots of ICO projects have been selling their tokens as a utility or digital coupon, or at least tried to turn their token into a digital good that does not have to follow the regulation process mandated for security tokens.

You have to consider that some jurisdictions are working on this gray area surrounding tokens. They tend to regulate them as a sale of shares, thus as financial securities. The unprecedented DAO attack and the ensuing wide media coverage encouraged regulators to take a deeper look in terms of regulatory control. In the future, it is most likely that ICOs will be regulated, whether tokens will be considered utilities or securities (more on that in Chapter 6, *Blockchain Legality, Compliance, and Regulation*).

Because the regulatory framework around ICOs is blurry, a similar fundraising method has been born that intends to benefit from both traditional IPO robustness and adherence with financial regulations such as those of the SEC in the US (the US SEC's equivalent institutions are the BaFin in Germany, the FINMA in Switzerland, and the AMF in France). This customized method is called STO and is technologically organized in the same way as an ICO (an issuance of tokens upon a distributed ledger).

The difference resides in the tokens sold that represent a specific regulated financial security, such as equity, debt, or derivative. The process of digitizing physical assets through blockchain-based tokens is called **tokenization**. Because companies operating an STO basically sell tokens representing a tradable financial asset, they have to comply even more rigorously than ICOs with financial institutions and requirements from regulatory bodies.

The upside, however, is that STOs still enjoy the digitized process, providing a seamless and transparent method to raise funds as well as ensuring digital value is transferred in a peer-to-peer and secured manner.

You should be aware that several terms exist in the blockchain world that designate fundraising methods through blockchain-based tokens. ICOs were the first one to emerge before the classification and nomenclature became more specific. Project leaders can now rely on STOs to issue digitally represented regulated financial securities, which can be subsided in different categories called ETOs or ITOs.

Do not get confused: although ETO and ITO are subsets of STO, which is itself a derived method of ICO, the main goal behind them all is the same: to raise money from individuals, companies, or institutions to carry out a project.

What is so revolutionary about ICOs?

ICOs are a true innovation in the traditional venture-funding model. Usually, a project could take months to be financed by investment funds and needs to have already been financed by angel investors, to have conducted strong marketing research, and have shown a real usefulness and need from customers.

Today, for an ICO to take off, all it takes is to write a nice description of a project through a so-called white paper, design a beautiful website, and showcase some drawings or pictures of the product. As simplistic as it sounds, some projects and pre-product start-ups actually raised a significant amount of money without any prototype or demonstration.

Many ICOs are launched every month, reaching new sky-high records in terms of funds raised. According to ICObench.com, a rating and listing website for ICOs, the biggest ICO ever was completed in May 2018 by EOS, who raised $4 billion to build a blockchain platform enabling the development, hosting, and execution of decentralized applications. The following is a screenshot of top ICOs by the value of sold tokens:

Top ICOs by the value of sold tokens	
#1 EOS	$4,197,956,135
#2 Telegram Open Network	$1,700,000,000
#3 BITFINEX	$1,000,000,000
#4 TaTaTu	$575,000,000
#5 Dragon	$320,000,000

If you're interested in checking out ICOs, you can navigate through the following websites:

- https://icobench.com/
- https://icorating.com/
- https://www.smithandcrown.com/
- https://www.coinschedule.com/
- https://www.cryptocompare.com/

Summary

In conclusion, ICOs are innovative ways to finance a project. They shift the crowdfunding method as we know it today into a decentralized and transparent way of raising money through an unlimited number of investors. Throughout the chapter, we established how effective it is for project leaders seeking leverage to advance the development of their blockchain-based application.

We showed how Ethereum enabled many dApps to be developed and tokens to be issued through their platform, increasing the democratization of ICOs. Also, we mentioned the story of the DAO, a groundbreaking practice to run an investment fund between individuals in a decentralized manner, which unfortunately suffered a massive hack during its ICO and attracted the attention of the US SEC and other financial authorities.

To this extent, we will touch upon an economic and social overview of blockchain in the next chapter. This will help us embrace a larger spectrum and avoid the common misconceptions and clichés that the latest effervescence has strengthened. We will then find out how global regulatory bodies are behaving and what actions public institutions have taken to keep up with the technological advancements brought by blockchain.

Section 2: Blockchain in Practice, Insights, and Achievements

In the first section, we covered what blockchain is and how it works. Now let's review how it can be applied in the real world, discover some use cases and realizations, and illustrate achievements across different industries. After reading this section, as a C-Level executive, you should be able to think of and define use cases for your own industry.

This section comprises of the following chapters:

- Chapter 5, *An Economic and Historical Approach of Blockchain*
- Chapter 6, *Blockchain Legality, Compliance, and Regulation*
- Chapter 7, *Blockchain for the Business World and Achievements*
- Chapter 8, *Future Outlook for Blockchain*

5
An Economic and Historical Approach of Blockchain

Now that you grasp the general and technical concepts of a blockchain, let's understand the fundamental problem blockchain tries to solve and how it came to us. Adopting a social and economic approach to understand blockchain can be very helpful to recognize projects that have a solid foundation and identify business opportunities.

With new technologies such as blockchain, we can imagine the next Uber relying on a distributed and decentralized infrastructure, where full remuneration would go to drivers and small fees retrieved to run the blockchain and reward the nodes empowering the network. In fact, that is what is already developing Eva, a blockchain-based Uber-like startup that has truly decentralized how drivers and customers interact to provide car-sharing services. But the case of Uber is just the tip of the iceberg. The centralized economies of scale scheme of today's collaborative platforms will be truly disrupted and evenly flattened between service providers and consumers, thanks to blockchain.

Decentralized environments are where blockchains have the most impact and where benefits are the biggest. Furthermore, until we reach such a kind of deconcentration between economic actors, institutions, and individuals, there is still time for blockchain to reach industrialization and user-friendliness.

In this chapter, we will focus on learning the reason behind the popularity of Bitcoin and other cryptocurrencies. We will approach these digital assets through an economic lens, understanding their underlying value and the upheaval they brought for capitalism. The following insights will give you the fundamentals to harness a global picture of blockchain's fulfillment. We shall also understand digital payment systems, the technical limitations of blockchain, and why it can be perceived as the ultimate layer of a more collaborative economy.

This chapter addresses the following topics:

- The economic global picture
- Blockchain as a missing tool for a collaborative economy
- Exchanging value in the digital world

The economic global picture

There have always been issues regarding trust between people. Using this as context, we created central authorities that can state the truth, and middlemen who can facilitate certain actions. This is part of the social contract: to solve trust issues between one another, there must be rules ensured by entities to which people must give up part of their freedom.

In most democracies, powers in the state are separated from centralized entities that govern the citizens: judicial, executive, and legislative. Each one has control over the other to avoid the abuse of power. But that is sometimes not enough to avoid wrongdoings or mistakes and keep the system entirely power balanced.

So, how can we achieve trust between individuals without trusted third parties?

Bitcoin provided the first answer in 2008 but the story dates back to before our era, 3,600 years ago, when our ancestors made use of different materials and natural elements as a means of exchange. The first identified form of money was cauris—little shells that were used by several tribes and nations across Asia, Africa, and Oceania to trade with each other. The following image shows a cauri:

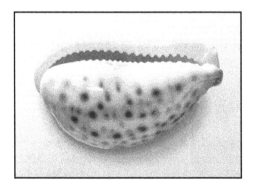

Just like money today, cauris were seen as a sign of wealth and prosperity. Around 600 BC, we started using gold minted coins as a primary medium of payment. Gold has every characteristic any monetary unit needs to have: it is rare, recognizable, and portable and, because of this, it has an intrinsic value.

Gold has since then been a standard. This was true until the modern age and particularly until the Bretton Woods Conference in 1944, where the United Nations reshaped the world monetary system and agreed on the dollar becoming the world's reserve currency, obliging other countries to align their currency to the dollar.

Money is trust

In 1971, Richard Nixon suspended the convertibility of the dollar into gold and forced every government to back their own currency. What was left was only trust and paper money, the so-called fiat money.

Somehow, the paradigm shift worked. People trusted their government to back bunches of paper, being told that it was actual money. Today, we still rely on these pieces of paper to pay for goods and services although they have no intrinsic value. Buying a coffee with a simple coin of metal is made possible because we trust our governments to sustain these coins and papers as the principal means of payment.

We are in a straightforward psychological pattern: because everybody uses euro, dollar, or yuan, these payment instruments have grown in value in the eyes of individuals that are willing to participate in economic life. And the more people that acknowledge the euro, dollar, or yuan as several means of payment, the more value they gain.

You have to understand that this is one of many accusations made against Bitcoin. When the European Central Bank says that Bitcoin is not money (`https://www.ecb.europa.eu/explainers/tell-me/html/what-is-bitcoin.en.html`), why would the bills and pennies be considered as such since they have no intrinsic value? If everybody entrusts Bitcoin to be the principal medium of payment, the evolution toward a new decentralized trustless payment system would automatically occur.

A decentralized digital payment system

Nowadays, all of the paper money is mainly stored in big banking databases. When you transfer money to someone, you just input an amount on your device to be sent to the other person. This is just a matter of movement of digits in a database that is owned by the bank.

Neither gold nor paper is moving between banks. Conclusion: Banks are digital payment systems enabling and securing money transfers from one individual to another. And, if you were wondering, PayPal is similar; it is a fully integrated digital payment system centralizing and storing money on its own servers.

Bitcoin is also a digital payment system but the principal difference is that it's not owned by any third party—no authority, no entity, no regulation, and no bank. Mark my words, when transferring money through your bank, you rely on it to carry out the verification of funds and to transfer to the right account. Since Bitcoin is not proprietary, the verification and the transfers are done in a decentralized manner through the Bitcoin network, thanks to cryptography and a consensus protocol.

Moreover, the decentralized feature of the Bitcoin network eliminates a single point of failure. Imagine your bank being hacked by a malicious group or person that could take over the data stored in the bank's servers and erase or modify it. With Bitcoin relying on the nodes of the network to store the history of every transaction and on cryptographic hashes to secure every block of the blockchain, it becomes unhackable and unalterable.

Bitcoin – a digital currency or gold 2.0?

The real difference with fiat currencies is that Bitcoin cannot be created from thin air. Dollars or euros are currencies that can be respectively issued by the **Federal Reserve** (**FED**) or the **European Central Bank** (**ECB**) at their discretion. Bitcoin, on the other hand, cannot be generated upon a unilateral decision. It is a scarce digital asset, only created through a predefined algorithm and cryptography, mathematics and a vast network of computers.

We should emphasize that what made gold valuable for 3,000 years is the effort endorsed by the people to dig it out. Bitcoin relies on the same characteristic. For a transaction to be validated, the network and, more specifically, the miners have to find a cryptographic hash that takes approximately 10 minutes to be found.

Once it is found, the network is rewarded with new Bitcoins poured into the system. It costs electricity, chips, and materials to be able to run and find the hash, just as it costs picks, shovels, and effort from the miners to unearth an ounce of gold.

Anybody can send money with Bitcoin. Compared to traditional bank transfers, it takes 10 minutes for the fund to be transferred and 60 minutes for the transaction to become unalterable.

In the Bitcoin blockchain, it takes 10 minutes for a block A to be validated by the miners and added to the chain. If five blocks are validated afterward (that is, 50 minutes later), the probability to erase the transactions in block A by a miner with 30% of the network's computing power decreases to under 1%. This period is a measure of how secure a transaction is. The more blocks validated after a transaction, the more secure it is.

Distance, acquaintance, and trust are meaningless variables for the transfer to happen properly between two individuals. Also, no bank account is needed to process the transfer: what you need is an internet connection and a Bitcoin wallet. A Bitcoin wallet is a digital wallet that can be created on `bitcoin.com` to send and receive Bitcoin. Here is a screenshot of a Bitcoin wallet:

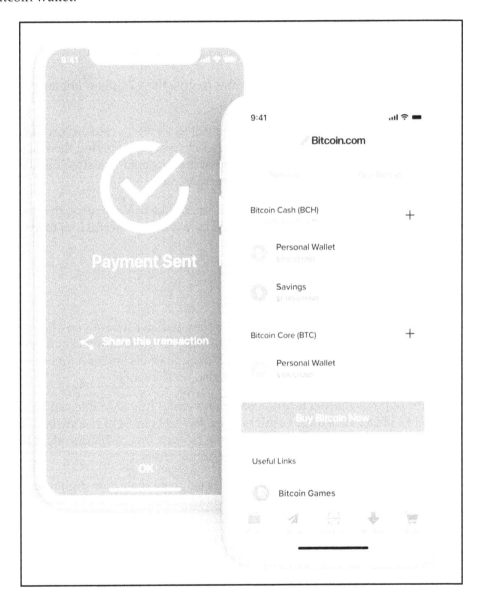

Investment product or real solution for the unbanked?

Since the hype in 2017, especially within the financial realm, Bitcoin has been seen by the public as a speculative class of assets. The wild ups and downs of the USD/BTC pair attracted money sharks and traders from global financial places. Bitcoin's fame was propelled by new *crypto-millionaires* and by traders' success stories. But this unsavory side of Bitcoin hides the real impact that it's trying to make in the world.

The first issue that is attempting to solve Bitcoin is to give the 1.7 billion unbanked people of this planet a frictionless means of payment.

When people from the richest countries see Bitcoin solely as an investment product, a large part of Bitcoin's community sees it as a digital currency eventually giving them access to digital payments and money transfers at a small cost and instantaneously. This is even truer for developing countries showing high corruption rates.

When people start to fear and mistrust their government like in Venezuela, they rely on cryptocurrencies as a promising alternative. We can see it as a powerful tool to avoid corruption, bankruptcy, and lack of transparency.

Adverse governments

Having such a digital payment system enabling money transfer without any bank account is one of the reasons for governments to dislike Bitcoin. The government claims that Bitcoin is mainly used for terrorism and access to Darknet drug markets and as a money-laundering mechanism. But we stress that cash is also used as such.

In fact, any means of payment that is untraceable and easily transportable can be used as such. Governments' objective is to go cashless to be able to both fight money laundering by tracking any value transfer online as well as enclose citizens in a cashless system to prevent large and sudden cash drains during potential economic crises.

A possible shift in the future for the governments is to create their own digital currency. This would mean a cashless system used by everybody but still controlled by a central authority. Note that, if governments choose a centralized way of controlling money supply and movements across the network, that is not a blockchain-based currency, it is a just a centralized coin, just as it is today.

This is an important point: thanks to the blockchain, Bitcoin provides monetary sovereignty outside government policy. That is why a lot of developing countries such as Venezuela, Zimbabwe, Nigeria, or South Africa are deeply opening up to cryptocurrencies in general.

Technical limits of Bitcoin

One remaining technical challenge for Bitcoin is scalability. Today, the Bitcoin blockchain can settle four to seven transactions per second, when Visa can handle around 2,000. Bitcoin's ultimate goal is to allow anybody to transfer money at a very low cost, really quickly, and anywhere in the world. Because it needs computational power to process a transaction, the fees per transaction are today too high to enable somebody to pay for a coffee with Bitcoin.

Hopefully, initiatives from the Bitcoin community to solve these problems are emerging and one technology known as the Lightning Network has been gaining attention. It is most likely that, in the future, the Bitcoin blockchain will be able to process a million transactions per second, becoming a fast, costless, and efficient payment system.

The Lightning Network is a layer implemented on the Bitcoin blockchain to enable fast and cheap transactions between individuals. Currently in the beta version, it works by allowing two parties to create a payment channel, basically a *common* wallet in which both parties deposit a certain amount. When the two parties transact, they update the amount assigned to each of them. When they eventually close the payment channel, each balance in the wallet is allocated accordingly to each party.

Blockchain as the missing tool for a collaborative economy

Other challenges are rising for Bitcoin but it has already proven what it is capable of and what issues it is solving. By aiming to provide a digital payment system for the 1.7 billion unbanked people, Bitcoin has shown the world that cryptography, consensus protocol, and decentralized databases are powerful enablers for a paradigm shift rendering the power to the crowd instead of a given central authority or third party.

"We need better cross-border payments ... because it's good for development, it's good for financial inclusion, so Bitcoin can help us."

- Benoit Coeure, European Central Bank executive board member in January 2018

In a world where the social, circular, and collaborative economy is flourishing, having a technology that allows anybody to share, trade, pay for, or sell anything within a secured and transparent network seems to be the missing piece of Jeremy Rifkins' *The Zero Marginal Cost Society*, 2014 (`http://www.thezeromarginalcostsociety.com/pages/The-Book.cfm`), a society empowered by collaborative behaviors, emerging technologies, and almost-free goods and services.

Actually, it is worth observing that an interesting coincidence happened in 2009 surrounding the expansion of the collaborative economy triggered by companies such as Uber and the development of distributed ledger technologies such as blockchain. Arising technologies such as 3D printing, the **Internet of Things** (**IoT**), or **artificial intelligence** (**AI**) transform current vertical schemes toward models where value is shared more directly, all of this being facilitated by digital platforms acting as a cornerstone of the *common* pattern of the new economy.

The energy industry is one clear example where consumers are now confounded with producers to become *prosumers*, using renewable sources of energy to provide power locally and efficiently. The same shift applies for education, where knowledge is shared between one another, and every other industry fed with capitalism, top-down approaches, and oligopolistic situations.

Decentralization - but why?

Many press releases and articles present Uber-like companies as innovative projects that have disrupted traditional business models, most of the time concluding the analysis with true decentralization being the final step—as if a decentralized economy was the ultimate goal.

As a decision maker, you should realize that what is missing in these analyses is that **decentralization is not a goal but a means**—a means to achieve a massive collaboration between individuals without the need for a central entity. The goal is to be able, as an individual or a company, to thrive and collaborate without friction, to produce and exchange value in a peer-to-peer manner, and to bring forward social benefits rather than financial profits.

With today's shift of consumption patterns induced by digital ubiquity, and with the rise of what we call **uberization**, it is more and more important for organizations to rethink their mode of operation, to answer the need for proximity and transparency sought by their final users.

 Uberization refers to digital platforms that facilitate peer-to-peer transactions between individuals and service providers.

Uber and Airbnb, as pioneers, quickly realized that the under-utilized assets and human resources of traditional companies could be overcome through digital tools. Uberization also refers to the collaborative economy with the first platforms that put into direct contact customers and service providers, thereby massively connecting people together and allowing them to exchange value, knowledge, expertise, service, assets, and much more.

But on our path to massive decentralization, it feels like several important intermediaries are remaining, including the platforms themselves. The collaborative economy is removing original monopolies for digital-native pervasive companies that rely more on data collection than profit margin to achieve growth.

Blockchain – the ultimate layer

What does blockchain have to do with all of this?

Well, blockchain can be seen as a layer that could eventually replace these platforms, granting control and power to the crowd but still allowing individuals to act responsibly and collaboratively. With blockchain, we could gain sovereignty over its data, trade its know-how to a counterpart, and exchange value with a peer, all without any intermediary.

Blockchain and distributed ledger technologies foster a participative, inclusive, and collaborative ecosystem, bringing transparency and security in a decentralized environment. They act as an instrument used to flatten processes and allow widespread collaboration for decision-making through its intrinsic incentive mechanism. We can quite easily draw parallels between issues discussed in *The Zero Marginal Cost Society* and the characteristics of a blockchain.

According to the author, Jeremy Rifkin, more and more companies are organized collectively (cooperative societies, for example). Just as a community is handled and managed by its members in a consensual manner, blockchain relies on the network to perform value transfer and information recording. The process is no longer descending and rigid but collaborative and flexible. Rifkin also predicts access to goods and services will be favored over ownership and collaboration over competition. The inner characteristic of a blockchain is that it is not owned by anyone and that it is distributed across all of the participants that work together toward a common truth. With this kind of mechanics, members can **cooperate in a trustless environment** where transparency and security are ensured thanks to cryptography.

But most importantly, blockchain is disruptive in the way that it enables value exchange in the digital world.

Exchanging value in the digital world

In the digital world, the million dollar question is: *how do you ensure that one digital asset cannot be replicated?*

To answer this question, it is important to understand that the internet was built to exchange information. This information is copied from computer to computer, replicated across the network. Each bit of data that goes through a node can be replicated or stored. In other words, once a piece of information is injected into the internet, it replicates and spreads quickly through the network that erases its uniqueness. This is how information transmission works—by replication.

The problem is that, in commercial transactions, we do not pass along information for free; we transact value that shouldn't be replicated. If I send you a dollar, I'm not supposed to hold it anymore because if I did, it would be worthless. Hence, value should be transferred as a move, not a copy. Any kind of value, including money, should be involved: land titles, car registration documents, copyrights, exclusive contracts, or company shares. Because value cannot be spent twice, blockchain ensures that **double-spending** is prevented in the digital world.

With blockchain, the internet of value was born. In the collaborative economy, only centralized platforms such as Uber and Airbnb secure the transfer of value from one individual to another. They ensure that the money you spent for a fare or renting a flat cannot be spent twice. This double-spending problem is one of the most complex challenges in the digital world.

The internet was built to exchange information that's copied from computer to computer, erasing the uniqueness out of it, because transmission works by replication. With blockchain, value is transferred like a move, not a copy, and this is what is needed for the collaborative economy to thrive in the digital age.

Summary

Hopefully, throughout this chapter, you understood what kind of social and economic concepts blockchain entails. From a modern currency to a digital payment system, we explained how Bitcoin has been playing the role of economic turmoil and how it now threatens some well-established public policies. We covered the main impact that Bitcoin is trying to achieve by giving money access to unbanked people and the technical limits it faces to do so. Eventually, we addressed a bigger challenge that blockchain can foster, the fulfillment of a more collaborative and responsible economy.

In the next chapter, we will stand alongside regulatory bodies and financial authorities to understand how governments and public institutions are facing the technological upheaval brought by blockchain and cryptocurrencies. We will see what legal, tax, and accounting aspects should be taken into consideration, as a decision maker, to achieve a blockchain project.

6
Blockchain Legality, Compliance, and Regulation

For any kind of blockchain-related project, whether it is creating a blockchain, using a Blockchain-as-a-Service solution, developing an application, or issuing a token, an evaluation of risks and opportunities has to be conducted by all the stakeholders who are involved.

In fact, there are specific scopes such as profitability, capacity, and cost that have to be adopted by a decision maker, but that would not be enough to secure a project. As the blockchain environment is fast-moving, many jurisdictions fail to frame cryptoassets and blockchains through laws and regulations properly. This chapter focuses on blockchains through the lens of legality, accounting, taxes, compliance, and regulations. We will legally define what a blockchain and a cryptocurrency is in the eyes of the law, and how this new technology and the digital assets it is generating have been handled by authorities worldwide. As a decision maker, you must be aware of the complex regulatory framework surrounding blockchain, and especially cryptoassets.

In any case, domestic regulators try to tackle challenges that are brought about by blockchain and cryptoassets until a global coordination is set to align regulations and taxonomy for a better and more comprehensive framework. For instance, in July 2018, the **Financial Stability Board** (**FSB**), whose role is to establish and coordinate the work of national financial authorities at an international level, published a report (`http://www.fsb.org/wp-content/uploads/P160718-1.pdf`) in response to the G20 that the Ministers of Finance held a few months earlier. This report identified metrics for monitoring the financial stability implications of cryptoasset markets, introduced support for ICO investors, and measured the exposure to cryptoassets that banks faced.

It is one of the first supranational initiatives that was launched to raise global awareness and provide education of cryptoassets and blockchain. This initiative will most certainly be followed by several efforts from such institutions to establish regulations and standards for this new technology at a worldwide level in the upcoming years.

In this chapter, we will cover the following topics:

- Laying the groundwork
- How to legally define a blockchain
- How to legally define tokens and other cryptoassets
- Overview of regulation frameworks
- Overview of accounting frameworks

Laying the groundwork

As of June 2019, we witnessed several initiatives to regulate, define, and frame tokens and blockchains in terms of laws and tax across the globe at different levels of power in the states. It is important to note that every jurisdiction has its own degree of awareness, its own degree of ambition to control the technology and its assets, its own way to gather information, and its own manner to make a decision about the ecosystem. In this fashion, risks and opportunities regarding a project's perimeter will mainly depend on the territory in which it is implemented.

As a decision maker, there are many questions around a blockchain-based project whose answers will mostly depend on external factors such as the jurisdiction and territory, but also on internal factors such as the sector, business size, and target clients. For instance, there is no universal answer to the following question: *What regulation should the blockchain project abide to?* The answer is rather local regarding the implementation of the project in a crypto-friendly or crypto-skeptic environment. Indeed, blockchain and cryptocurrencies are perceived very differently according to the region they are implemented in. It is important to note that the main concerns from authorities and institutions are not toward blockchain itself but rather the assets that it is generating, that is, the so-called tokens tied to the blockchain.

A project's appropriate compliance will also depend on which business lines are affected by the project, which subsidiaries are concerned, and in which place. Then comes the question of how to handle tax issues such as benefits for R&D tax reduction and, more importantly, issues regarding the accountability and depreciation of the blockchain project. Several countries have significantly advanced cryptoassets accounting in financial statements and made such topics a real concern for many companies. Eventually, a compliant blockchain project is also a project that has taken care of other regulations, such as data protection (**General Data Protection Regulation** (**GDPR**) in the European Union), a customers' identity (**Know Your Customer** (**KYC**) policy), and criminality prevention (**Anti Money Laundering** (**AML**) and **Combating the Financing of Terrorism** (**CFT**)).

In these circumstances, we shall cleanse the blockchain environment by providing suitable definitions regarding the neologism surrounding the ecosystem, such as *token*, *cryptocurrency* or *cryptoasset*, in order to qualify them properly. What exactly should we understand when we're talking about a token, a digital asset, or a cryptocurrency? What does it mean for authorities and institutions now that value can be transferred digitally without replication? In the end, by stating the definition of these terms, we can restrict their meaning and eventually apply rules and laws.

How to legally define a blockchain

A blockchain is a combination of a protocol, a peer-to-peer network, and information flowing through a database in a cryptographic manner. The state of New York defines blockchain as follows:

> *"It is a distributed ledger technology, which is a mathematically secured, chronological, and decentralized consensus ledger or database, whether maintained via internet interaction, peer-to-peer network, or otherwise used to authenticate, record, share, and synchronize transactions in their respective electronic ledgers or databases, and business entities that develop distributed ledger technology"*
> (http://www.ncsl.org/research/financial-services-and-commerce/the-
> fundamentals-of-risk-management-and-insurance-viewed-through-the-lens-
> of-emerging-technology-webinar.aspx).

The main question that arises from the core definition of blockchain is about data privacy, especially for public blockchains in which transactions are disclosed. Because information is stored in the blockchain, there is a need for a secured and tough policy to manage this data and avoid leakage and corruption. Authorities are rarely intrusive of this topic, although they try to understand what it implies and what kind of data is flowing through the blockchain.

Blockchain, as a sole instrument, will only be questioned on the data it incorporates, but one regulation must be taken into account when a project is implemented in the European Union: GDPR. This regulation, that was put into effect as of May 2018, aims to protect a customer's data and encourage companies to manage it properly.

Blockchain and GDPR

Ironically, GDPR states that data should be handled in a centralized manner, whereas blockchain tends to process information in a decentralized way. Also, GDPR provides the right to erasure, the right to rectification, and the principle of data minimization. These rights and principles are, at first sight, not compatible with those of blockchain.

Several European authorities, such as the European Commission, through the creation of the Blockchain Observatory, are currently working on the most suitable designs to bring answers and best practices to the table. Meanwhile, decision makers should remain cautious: the paradox between GDPR and blockchain becomes a challenge if the project is entirely supported by a public blockchain. The more decentralized and transparent your blockchain project is, the more conditions should be respected to comply with GDPR. Because information flows transparently on the ledger within a public infrastructure, no personal data can be exposed.

How to legally define tokens and other cryptoassets

Cryptoassets, cryptocurrencies, tokens, and coins are all terms that often bring confusion within the ecosystem. Some of them mean the same thing, while others are subsets. However, they all have something in common: they have a digital value. Let's try to define these terms in a relevant way to facilitate the applicability of a given regulation and clarify the terminology.

Cryptocurrencies

Cryptocurrencies are either tokens or coins. A cryptocurrency can be defined as an **independent** digital currency where the issuance, the transaction validation process, the availability of the application, and the governance are totally independent. It is opposed to a digital currency, where all the characteristics are defined and administered by a central authority.

Cryptocurrency is any blockchain-based token that is solely used as a means of payment and has enough liquidity and sufficient acceptance to be considered as a material to buy or sell goods and services (see `Chapter 5`, *An Economic and Historical Approach to Blockchain*). We can put the following tokens into this category (not exhaustive):

- Bitcoin
- Ethereum
- Bitcoin Cash
- Litecoin
- Monero

Non-cryptocurrencies

Non-cryptocurrencies, also referred to as blockchain-based tokens, embrace a much broader concept than cryptocurrencies because they are not only used as a means of payment. A token intrinsically has a vast and abstract definition and can designate a cinema ticket, a discount voucher, or a chip in an online game.

Most of these tokens are not blockchain-based tokens, so we shall call them crypto tokens when we talk about tokens in a blockchain. Cryptographic tokens are digital assets that can be transferred from peer-to-peer (like cryptocurrency) but have specific characteristics attached to them. Data is incorporated in the issued token, which confer some rights to the owner.

 Ether is both a cryptocurrency (it is used as a means of payment and it has a value shaped according to market demand) and a non-cryptocurrency (Ether allows the service provided by the platform to be used).

In most jurisdictions, these non-cryptocurrencies tokens are gaining attention because they are assets that do not fall under the current regulation. We can split these tokens into two categories, although they can be split into more according to some jurisdictions. Refer to `Chapter 4`, *ICOs and Tokenized Fundraising Methods*, for more details:

- **Security token:** The token gives the user the right to perceive dividends or profits from the product or service.
- **Utility token:** The token is used as the right to purchase a product or a service and has no financial right attached to it.

All the external factors related to tax, accounting, and legality, are defined based on the previous definition in many jurisdictions. With this in mind, you can state whether the underlying token in your blockchain project is a security or a utility and therefore establish a plan to comply with the law.

Overview of regulation frameworks

Since the hype of ICOs in 2017, many authorities and institutions took action to establish a legal framework and general guidelines. Since the DAO failed to see this (see `Chapter 4`, *ICOs and Tokenized Fundraising Methods*), the US SEC undertook efforts to fit the new asset class into US laws.

The case of the DAO is significant because it caused an investigation by the US SEC into defining tokens as financial securities or utilities. The SEC released its report of investigation in July 2017 (one month after the DAO's failures) stating that DAO tokens should have been subject to security laws because they were labeled as such. This was one of the first initiatives toward regulating cryptoassets, at least in the US. The SEC advanced this immense task to a globally agreed perspective on tokens and gave out a starting point for categorizing them using the Howey test in order to determine the classification of a cryptoasset.

With this first initiative, the SEC triggered concerns from other institutions from overseas who started to pay attention to tokens and, more broadly to ICOs. It occurred to them that an ICO was financially disruptive because it allowed any project leader to raise funds quickly and costlessly, and for investors to invest directly and instantaneously in a project without paying fees to a venture capital firm, thus avoiding the current regulated funding scheme. Public institutions, associations, and authorities realized that there was work to undertake both to legally define the tokens issuance process as well as to protect the investors. Policies such as KYC and AML gained reinforcement to protect stakeholders from too risky and irresponsible investments and comply with regulatory bodies.

Because security tokens really look like traditional shares, they fall into the scope of a much-regulated domain where issuance and marketing are examined as an investor's identities, the purpose of the funds, and the related risks. In this fashion, authorities became really concerned with alerting people and investors about the potential danger of investing in an ICO, especially in security tokens. The Federal Financial Supervisory Authority in Germany released a note in June 2017, as well as the Financial Conduct Authority in the United Kingdom in April 2018, to investors regarding risks related to investing in ICOs.

The following is an overview of the countries that absolutely banned or implicitly banned cryptocurrencies from their jurisdiction:

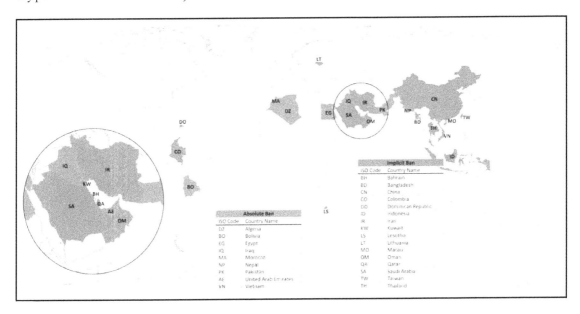

The following is an overview of tax laws, AML, and CFT standards:

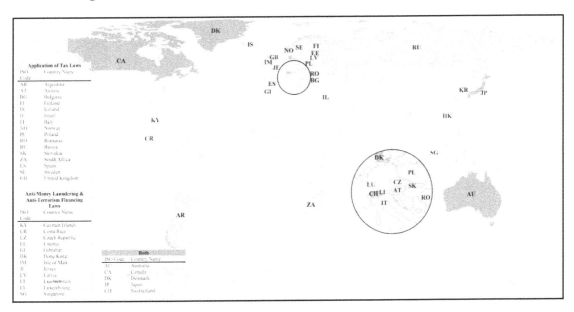

The following is an overview of the countries that have or are in the process of issuing their own national cryptocurrency:

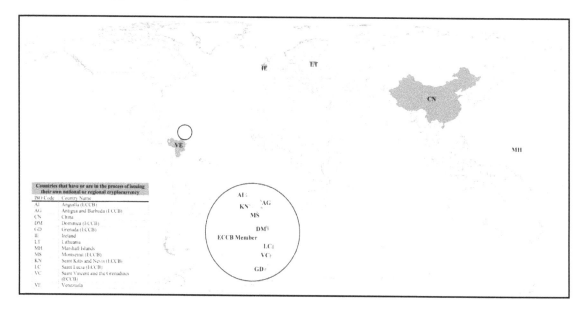

If you want to find out more about how regulations and policies are apprehended over the world, you can consult the following report, which was made by the US Library of Congress, at `https://www.loc.gov/law/help/cryptocurrency/cryptocurrency-world-survey.pdf`.

Overview of accounting frameworks

Given the ever-increasing number of ICOs being conducted, some institutions have raised questions regarding how to account tokens in the financial statements of a firm since we were dealing with a new class of assets.

If you are running a one-hundred-year-old firm selling cars and you are willing to issue tokens to allow people to purchase certain kinds of products or services, how would you proceed?

You would launch an ICO where you will sell newly created crypto tokens against, say, dollars. This is a case where you should consider the following questions:

- How would you account for the funds that were raised on your balance sheet?
- How would you account for the remaining tokens in your **profit and loss** (P&L) statement?

These questions are currently being discussed in several jurisdictions over the world. Switzerland has a very crypto-friendly attitude towards ICO and for accounting tokens without negatively affecting corporate tax. The city of Zug actually became the capital of the Crypto Valley, an ecosystem of blockchain entrepreneurs, startups, and incubators that attracted several famous blockchain companies, such as ConsenSys.

In France, unprecedented work has been done by the **Accounting Norms Authority** (**ANC**), who published a paper in December 2018 indicating that some tokens must be recorded in the balance sheet as debt or as turnover according to their qualification. On top of that, the ANC was the first institution in the world to introduce cryptoassets in the domestic chart of accounts.

This work is the result of previous interrogations that have been made by other authorities. In Australia, the **Australian Accounting Standard Board** (**AASB**) who oversees the country's reporting standards, sent a paper in December 2016 (https://www.aasb.gov.au/admin/file/content102/c3/AASB_ASAF_DigitalCurrency.pdf) to the **International Accounting Standard Board** (**IASB**) arguing that a more defined standard was needed for digital currencies and other intangible assets.

According to the AASB, cryptoassets shouldn't be considered as cash or cash equivalent, nor as financial instruments, because they do not represent a treasury flow in the financial statement (according to the IAS 7 norm definitions) and because there is no underlying contractual relationship. The AASB pointed out that, on the other hand, a cryptocurrency meets the definition of another norm, the IAS 38, stating that it should be considered as an intangible asset because it is an identifiable non-monetary asset without physical substance.

Aware of this disruptive topic, the **International Federation of Accountants** (**IFAC**) wrote a report (https://www.ifac.org/system/files/publications/files/Blockchain-Slide-Deck_0.pdf) in May 2018 to accountancy firms about blockchain's impact on accounting principles. Surprisingly, the note stipulates that blockchain will have a positive impact on accountants by providing full visibility on audit trails, greater performance for reporting tools, and enhanced monitoring through smart contracts.

Summary

In this chapter, we started by understanding why, as a decision maker, it is important to take regulatory frameworks into consideration when launching a blockchain project, especially since 2017's hype that aroused public authorities' attention. Legal questions need to be addressed as there is more and more concerns from regulatory bodies towards blockchain. We established legal definitions on blockchain's terminology and neologism in order to fundamentally grasp what cryptoassets, cryptocurrencies, and tokens are in the eyes of the law. We ended this chapter by looking at the different initiatives that have been taken worldwide in terms of legality and accounting.

Now that you have technical, economic, and legal knowledge about blockchain and cryptoassets, in the next chapter, we'll dive into the business world to discover what applications have been made out of this new technology, what disruptive services and products have been launched, and what perspective we are to expect.

Blockchain for the Business World and Achievements

7

In this chapter, we will illustrate the potential of blockchain through several applications that have been implemented in various sectors of the economy. We will discover how blockchain disrupted businesses, bringing transparency and enabling traceability across supply chains, how cryptoassets are redesigning business models with tokenization, bringing liquidity and digital representation of any given physical asset, and, finally, how smart contracts can replace intermediaries and offer seamless transactions between companies and individuals.

Every case presented in this chapter starts with a business issue that enterprises meet and struggle to overcome while explaining how blockchain facilitates resolving the issue. This chapter will illustrate which existing projects and initiatives were created to respond to these business issues.

We shall go through the following topics:

- Authentication and trustworthiness
- Interoperability
- Traceability
- Automation, disintermediation, and self-organization
- Digital identities
- Financial securities and fundraising
- Digital uniqueness

Authentication and trustworthiness

Many companies have already been confronted with forged releases on their behalf about their financial health and strategic choices, especially in the digital age where monitoring and preventing fake communications has become more and more difficult. This reality is very common for enterprises whose official and sensitive documents such as financial statements are attentively observed by shareholders, creditors, banks, investors, and public institutions.

Document fraud, in general, is a serious issue for public institutions and governments. In France, it represented an €8 billion loss in 2017, according to the National Delegation to Combat Fraud (DNLF) (`https://www.lejdd.fr/Economie/la-caisse-des-depots-engie-edf-et-la-poste-sallient-dans-la-blockchain-3898162`). This problem was taken over by KeeeX, a French startup that developed a product to allow companies and individuals to certify any given file. Founded in 2014, they use the Bitcoin blockchain to seal any kind of digital file. When someone needs to verify the authenticity of that file, they use the KeeeX application to reveal its genuineness.

The explanation is that companies and individuals can rely on blockchain to ensure that electronic documents and data can be trusted because it was recorded by the right person in the first place. As a reminder, blockchain is a sort of distributed database in which data is timestamped and recorded in a consensual manner. Because this registry is transparent, it allows users to browse history to retrieve a transaction or information seamlessly. By design, these characteristics are very useful to authenticate data sources and trustworthiness.

KeeeX's product is a very powerful and simple example to understand hash functions and distributed ledger technology. The process starts with the original file being encrypted with a hash function that returns a cryptographic number. This hash is sent through a transaction on the Bitcoin blockchain, timestamped, and appended to a block. This means that, whenever someone claims to be the author of the original file, a simple search of the cryptographic number into the blockchain returns its timestamp and address. With this information, it becomes straightforward to point out the rightful issuer, the genuine document, and the date it was submitted.

Designers, architects, writers, and artists actually face the same problem as large businesses: their work is valuable and it becomes harder to protect it to prevent theft and replication.

Blockchain in the music industry

The case of songwriters and producers is self-evident: today, music is mainly consumed in digital format. According to the **Recording Industry Association of America** (**RIAA**), online streaming platforms generate 75% of the industry's revenue. Copyright theft has become mainstream and music piracy continues to torment the entire music industry, especially because of the increasing popularity of these platforms.

The RIAA estimates that music piracy costs $12.5 billion annually and it gets harder for the creators to get paid for their works accordingly, as there are complex money flows induced by the presence of many intermediaries. Actually, Rethink Music's study (`https://www.riaa.com/wp-content/uploads/2018/09/RIAA-Mid-Year-2018-Revenue-Report.pdf`) estimates that 20 to 50 percent of music payments don't make it to their rightful owners.

Hopefully, the rise of blockchain presents a solution to prevent copyright theft and ensure accurate payment to authors for their creations. The challenge here is to provide a digital signature attached to the song that links to the creator. Key encryption and hash functions also play an important role in this scheme to provide a unique identifier to the song or creation that, once recorded on the blockchain, becomes timestamped and verified as the artist's property.

Any further use of this song will be permanently recorded in the ledger, allowing tracing and tracking. Concretely, a blockchain-based music platform such as Ujo Music (`http://static1.squarespace.com/static/552c0535e4b0afcbed88dc53/t/55d0da1ae4b06bd4bea8c86c/1439750682446/rethink_music_fairness_transparency_final.pdf`) enables an artist to submit its creation on the platform, which will generate a hash out of it. This hash acts as proof to authenticate that this creation was submitted by this author at a specific time. The latter can establish the terms under which the creation may be used and the royalties associated with it.

Funds for licensing the creation then go directly to the author's wallet. Using blockchain in this peer-to-peer manner prevents the copyright and licensing abuse of digital songs submitted onto the platform. Several initiatives have seen the light in recent years to advance tangible solutions to these major problems. The most renowned besides Ujo Music (`https://ujomusic.com/`) are Mycelia (`http://myceliaformusic.org/`) and Mediachain (`http://www.mediachain.io/`), which was acquired by Spotify in 2017.

More broadly, intellectual property can benefit a great added value from blockchain which could serve as a platform upon which proper ownership of digital assets can be recorded.

Litigation on the origin and author of a creation could be resolved by referring to a tamper-proof timestamp indicating when exactly the idea was recorded. Consequently, blockchain can protect artists from thieves and infringers by authenticating their artworks, sketches, or drawings.

Leveraging the Internet of Things (IoT)

Blockchain and IoT are two emerging technologies that actually can come along together. Being implemented as a truly distributed system incorporating cryptographic algorithms, blockchain provides trust and security to the members of the network who cannot update information without the agreement of everyone else. Moreover, chained data makes it nearly impossible to modify the ledger. In this fashion, cybersecurity within IoT finds its interest in blockchain.

Sensors are usually installed in the periphery of the infrastructure and data is stored in its core, the so-called cloud. The challenge is that many enterprises wish to integrate intelligence right into the sensors, which as a result raises security questions. By authenticating sensors and terminals on the blockchain, we can implement the first level of security. Because every movement can be traced on the blockchain, the origin of the data can also be stated, that is, from which sensors it comes.

Silicon Valley's startup, Xage, came up with the idea of securing billions of devices on the blockchain to create a secure environment for them to operate. They provide a trustless mechanism for companies to ensure that their devices cannot be compromised. By connecting reliable devices to the blockchain it becomes easier to protect them from malicious intrusion and an unexpected hack.

The objective is to control the information flow between stakeholders, thanks to security timestamps appended on the servers. This kind of utilization of the distributed ledger technology might seem surprising as this is not its main function, but its purposes are wide enough to seek other means to solve business issues such as erasing a single point of failure.

The combination of IoT and blockchain is a truly disruptive approach as it integrates two promising technologies. It is important to stress that most of the projects launched using sensors and blockchain are not even in the pilot phase. Investments in IoT have exploded in several industries and IDC, a market research firm, forecasted the total amount to reach $1 trillion by 2022 (`https://www.idc.com/getdoc.jsp?containerId=prUS44596319`).

Because data recorded on the blockchain is verified and encrypted using cryptography, it is less prone to being hacked or changed without permission. Blockchain eliminates intermediaries, making it more efficient than many legacy systems and cybersecurity.

Interoperability

In some sectors such as banking or insurance, data is flowing between companies and regulators to be able to provide appropriate services to customers. Exchanging data between untrusted parties turns out to be a painful and complicated process, especially because strong regulations exercise caution regarding which kind of data is being transferred between entities.

In this context, it is hard to ensure that an individual's information can be shared properly, in accordance with laws and without friction. For instance, in the case of insurance, customers have to deliver attestations and certificates provided by third-parties institutions such as their unemployment agency, medical practitioners, school administration, or governmental bodies to prove the occurrence of a given event.

Blockchain can erase the friction, in this process, by allowing the exchange of data between entities upon the customer's consent. Once a first authorization of sharing personal credentials has been granted by the customer to the third-party institution, the insurer can then query the blockchain to retrieve this authorization as a license to access the customer's information held by the third party.

Practically, the third-party institution possesses specific data on the customer such as the birth date, social security number, diploma, health record, and many more that could be sent to the customer's public key through a cryptographic message recorded on the blockchain to prove its ownership.

When the insurer requests specific data to deliver compensation, for example, it can browse the blockchain to search for the public key of the customer. Once found, the insurer can tell which third party institution to consult to retrieve the data needed to render the service to the customer. This blockchain-based claim process radically improves the client experience by transforming the traditional claim process into an automated, secured, and seamless process for every stakeholder.

Moreover, data privacy stays guaranteed since personal information remains stored on every stakeholder's database without flowing through the blockchain.

In this process, the blockchain plays a role of a layer on which a given entity can exchange messages, including information on the type of data it owns upon an individual, to another entity and share the actual data privately according to the individual's consent.

Because no personal information can allegedly be communicated on the blockchain, claim registries have a disruptive way of proving certain characteristics without disclosing personal information.

Stratumn, a French prizewinning blockchain startup, is currently working on bringing interoperability among the banking and insurance sectors with a product called *Trace* that has been used by several European companies in the aforementioned manner.

Another example of how blockchain achieves interoperability can be illustrated with a case in the sports industry. Today, sports federations face two major problems:

- Difficulty in enlisting more licensees
- An increase in identity theft during sports events, especially in amateur games

Hurdles to enlist as a licensee, partly come from the subscription process, which is still paper-based for some federations and time-consuming, especially for people willing to practice several activities. With the combination of dematerialization and a public blockchain, users could easily share more information required to play sports as well as prevent identity theft during events.

For instance, we could subscribe to a specific sport by following a digital process through which we would share personal data and certificates to practice to the corresponding federation. When subscribing for another activity to another federation, we would only have to send our digital identity (their public key) to the new federation, which would look up the blockchain to notice that data has already been approved by another federation.

Such friction would be eradicated through a digital endorsement from the person who authorized sharing personal information by only presenting their digital identity to the new federation. This entire digital and blockchain-based process ensures that data is appropriately shared between entities and that no impersonation happens during sports events.

Not only insurance, banking, and sports industries can solve interoperability issues through blockchain. In fact, any sector in which competitors have converging interests but mistrust each other can rely on blockchains as a layer to make partitioned databases speak to each other **without disclosing personal or sensitive information**, to answer ultimately the most important problem—catering to the customer's requirements.

Traceability

In April 2019, the world's tenth-largest commercial food retailer, Albertsons (`https://stores.org/stores-top-retailers-2018/`), announced its involvement in IBM's Food Trust Blockchain to launch a pilot for tracking romaine lettuce, hence joining 79 other brands to the consortium such as Walmart, Nestle, and Unilever. The IBM Food Trust Blockchain is a modular and collaborative network solution gathering economic actors and aiming to tackle major problems within the commercial food chain, such as being able to identify the origin of dodgy products, the primary source of diseases and sanitary scandals, and enabling removal of infected products from retailers' stores without clearing the whole supply chain.

In the food industry, focus on safety is a priority and the traceability of a product has become paramount. In this context, many food producers, suppliers, and retailers are looking for a way to trace products. IBM's Food Trust Blockchain seems to have brought a relevant means to do so and has onboarded major players in the food supply chain including Topco, Wakefern, and Carrefour. Their customers can now use a mobile application to scan a QR code to retrieve information about a specific product—its origin, the producer's name, or the quality control certificates.

As of today, only a few products have been enjoying these services but these initiatives tend to enhance the food supply chain that is often criticized for its opacity and its lack of fairness toward producers.

Blockchains also improve the operational efficiency of the supply chains. Products moving along the process are often not tracked, which means that any problems that occur cannot be adequately isolated and investigated. With blockchain, transactions are documented permanently and monitored transparently, enabling the reduction of time delays and human mistakes.

It can also be used to monitor costs, labor, and even waste in emissions at every point in a supply chain. This has serious applications for understanding and controlling the real environmental impacts of products. Opposed to traditional databases, blockchain allows the possibility to master permissions of each information added to the ledger to ensure trust between stakeholders and obtain a single source of truth. Because responsibility is shared between each actor along the process, transparency plays a key role in this scheme.

Blockchain has the potential to disrupt the way food supply chains are handled, by accelerating the identification of tainted products, providing information on transportation conditions, and reducing losses due to deterioration. This decentralized mode of sharing information is made possible because each node of the network is represented by a single entity that has a predefined authority to validate transactions, to store the registry, or to use the service.

This mass coordination between competitors, suppliers, and clients in a competitive environment is a remarkable example of what a blockchain can achieve. Unfortunately, sometimes, mass coordination cannot be achieved with a blockchain alone and the carrier industry is a blatant example.

The carrier industry is a heterogeneous environment where ship owners, transporters, customs, and terminals must come together to ensure efficient logistic. Just like in the commercial food industry, blockchain has a role to play. There too, IBM perked up to propose a solution that was launched collaboratively with Maersk, the world's biggest carrier, in August 2018.

Their solution, called TradeLens, is dedicated to recording data on merchandise during its shipping journeys such as temperature or itinerary. This platform aims to share information on transit conditions and performance between actors, allowing them to adjust their resources according to ins and outs.

As promising as it sounds, TradeLens struggles to succeed because only a few companies joined the movement. Just like any project relying on a blockchain, the network effect is a very important component in the adoption process. As of today, TradeLens strived to onboard other carriers (`https://www.coindesk.com/ibm-blockchain-maersk-shipping-struggling`) to the platform. Some of them actually signed up to another competing platform called CargoSmart backed by Oracle, which uses blockchain to achieve similar objectives as TradeLens, namely, bringing trust and transparency in the sector.

In the end, if the logistic supply chain wants to become more effective by enhancing collaboration and transparency, only one platform should prevail because two separate projects will shatter the whole process and fragment the ecosystem.

In the automotive industry as well, blockchain has been thought of as a means to gather precious information along a process involving multiple parties and to improve synergies to fulfill customers' experience.

Ford, the world's fifth-largest car manufacturer according to the International Organization of Motor Vehicle Manufacturers (OICA) (`http://www.oica.net/wp-content/uploads/World-Ranking-of-Manufacturers-1.pdf`), has launched a consortium called the Mobility Open Blockchain Initiative (MOBI) in May 2018 with two other competitors, BMW and Renault.

This cluster aims to make mobility services more efficient and affordable and greener by promoting standards and accelerating the adoption of blockchain. They are currently developing a tool that could trace the maintenance history of a car, a kind of passport that would be readable by car dealers and garage owners to perform appropriate updates of worn parts.

The car's digital identity in this system is the cornerstone as it incorporates a lot of information such as the color, the model, the type of vehicle, or its constructor. Such a platform, where different actors update information on a given vehicle would erase painful processes of resale, transfer of ownership, and determination of accurate market value.

Moreover, the immutability provided by blockchain reduces mistrust between second-hand car resellers and buyers regarding the condition of the vehicle. With blockchain, tracking a vehicle's life is made possible and collaboration between actors strengthened.

Another prominent example of how traceability is achieved more efficiently through blockchain is in the diamond and jewelry industry, which is facing many frauds, forgeries, and robberies notably induced by a harrowing and risk-increasing paper-based certification process. Because the intrinsic value of an item is shaped according to its history and origin, provenance has become a serious matter in the luxury goods industry. These challenges were tackled in 2015 by Everledger, a leading emerging technology enterprise, providing a track and trace solution for diamonds using blockchain.

As of today, more than 2 million diamonds have been digitally represented and encrypted through their platform. Blockchain was implemented as a single source of truth for all stakeholders in the process without needing one entity to ensure that all information in the ledger is correct.

The record is visible to all participants, hence increasing confidence between actors and consumers. The solution is hosted on the IBM Blockchain Platform, which provides the IT infrastructure for the registry to be updated. Concretely, by involving several diamond certification houses around the world, they were able to create a unique identifier for each diamond, based on several characteristics such as its color, clarity, size, carat weight, and, of course, the micro-laser inscription written on the edge of the diamond and the GIA number, which serves as a link to a grading report of the stone.

Once this unique identifier or thumbprint is sent into the blockchain, it becomes easier for insurers to track the loss of the related stone and refund the customers, for law enforcement to identify fraud, and for online marketplaces to detect the sale of a stolen or a forged item.

Another sector worth illustrating with traceability is the energy industry, where many issues regarding **Guarantees of Origin** (**GO**), which label electricity from renewable sources of energy, remain. These certificates are issued by regulators and government bodies that ensure trust about the provenance of electricity.

This organization for delivering GO has several downsides acknowledged by major European energy actors (`http://resource-platform.eu/wp-content/uploads/files/downloads/RE-Source-Platform-Guideline-on-GOs-and-PPAs.pdf`) claiming a lack of transparency.

A few blockchain projects have seen the light in the past few years to overcome this issue and be able to issue a green certificate independently, without relying on public third parties. These projects were born by a pool of enterprises coming together to build a consortium and address important issues, not only regarding simplification and increased transparency of certificate-origin markets for renewable energy, but also regarding the grid of the future, the reduction of fraud, and the challenges for electric mobility.

This consortium, called the Energy Web Foundation, includes multiple affiliates and has launched an Ethereum-based platform called Tobalaba in 2017. The first application built on this platform is Origin EW whose goal is to track certified renewable energy kWh and integrate certificate markets to simplify and enhance the way customers purchase renewable energy. This decentralized application automatically records the provenance of renewable energy and tracks ownership information such as location, time, source type, and carbon emission.

Just like in commercial food, carrier, automotive, luxury goods, and energy industries, companies usually gather together around a consortium or a project where everyone contributes to create standards and facilitate information transfer. Never before have we seen such a degree of collaboration between competitors within the same industry. It is made possible because most of these actors believe in decentralization as a means for better coordination, improved efficiency, and cost-reduction through disintermediation.

Automation, disintermediation, and self-organization

So far, we have talked only about blockchain itself and how it solves authentication, interoperability, and traceability issues in different business areas. We've only addressed problems where decentralized and distributed databases combined with cryptographic algorithms and consensus protocols could advance value transfer and data sharing in a trustless environment to another level.

We showed that collaboration and coordination between competitors could be improved with a decentralized infrastructure empowered by a blockchain. We will now cover business issues that can be solved with smart contracts. As a reminder, smart contracts are computer programs that execute actions when certain conditions are met. They behave as a virtual person, performing actions under the respective code.

In `Chapter 3`, *Ethereum and Smart Contracts*, we illustrated how smart contracts work with the example of fizzy, Axa's application, which automatically triggers a refund to customers when their flight is behind schedule. In the previous sections, smart contracts were not needed because tamper-proof information and decentralization were sufficient features to answer the aforementioned business issues. However, to solve more complex problems and execute operations automatically and consensually, smart contracts are required.

Smart contracts for energy

Let's dive back into the energy sector again. Beyond being able to certify renewable energy's origin without third parties, tougher challenges have arisen in the past decade. As global warming surges as a concern, and with an estimated rise in temperature of 1.4 C° to 5.5 C° over the next century (`https://climate.nasa.gov/effects/`), never before have we been looking for a more sustainable, cleaner, and reusable source of energy.

The impact of climate change is gaining momentum much faster than was anticipated, while the shift from fossil fuels to cleaner energy is slow. Hopefully, innovations are being implemented to smoothly and intelligently achieve this transition.

Electrical smarter grids

The current *traditional method* of electricity supply is built on a centralized system operated by major energy and utility companies. It consists of a main grid in which energy is produced at large power stations and distributed to consumers through a wide transmission network. Although electrical grids are widespread, 1.4 billion people are still not connected to an electrical grid according to the Swedish Institute of International Affairs. The smaller grids (the microgrids) are linked to localized power sources in a decentralized pattern. For example, buildings of a given neighborhood with their own solar panels might be connected to nearby residences. Distributed energy resources combined with smart microgrids provide an intelligent production and energy transfer within a community.

Blockchain can play an active role in securing transactions between consumers and producers. To illustrate that, imagine an exchange platform where households and individuals could exchange their surplus of energy within a trading token-based system where the token serves as a means of payment.

The more electricity you produce and share, the more tokens you earn, and, as a sole consumer, you get the advantage to pay only for what you consume. All of it is empowered by a secure, transparent, and decentralized blockchain and smart contracts.

That is exactly what a neighborhood in Brooklyn has been achieving. This project, called the **Brooklyn Microgrid** (`https://www.brooklyn.energy/about`), is one of the first energy-related initiatives using blockchain. It was launched by LO3 Energy, a New York-based startup, to allow people to power their homes through a range of local renewable energy sources. People with their own solar panels can sell the surplus of electricity to their neighbors.

Blockchain and smart contracts intervene in this first peer-to-peer network for electricity to ensure an accurate record of transactions, a decentralized accounting and metering, and shared and transparent data to users of the network. In short, blockchain enables smart demand response management.

Initially, the Brooklyn Microgrid project targeted the regions that are not connected to their national grid by installing solar panels and batteries, which is an easy way to bring a basic amount of electricity to a village as long as the flexibility is managed accordingly. This is where blockchain and particularly smart contracts help; they secure energy transactions among users and producers. They provide a reliable, lower-cost digital platform for making, validating, recording, and settling energy transactions in real time across a localized and decentralized energy system.

What blockchain also unlocks is security. As modern electrical grids introduce computers, smart meters, and sensors, they can be prone to malicious intrusion or attacks. There are now cyber threats surrounding data management and transactions that blockchain can overcome. The fact that centralized power stations are perceived as potential targets for hackers is encouraging governments to accelerate the shift toward distributed energy resources, which decreases the risk of terrorist attacks.

The ultimate goal for an electrical grid is to become smart enough to grow the flexibility market and demand response market to balance the grid effectively and ultimately integrate more renewable energy.

A smart grid is supposed to be a combination of efficient power delivery (reliable, sustainable, and of high quality) and economically affordable per the needs of the user. With that in mind, blockchain, smart contracts, and IoT combined with embedded processing, real-time communications, and appropriate software, will definitely improve the reliability and efficiency of the grid and the network. The grid of the future will track energy generation and consumption monitored by connected objects, executed by smart contracts, and recorded on a blockchain.

Smarter electric mobility

Another topic related to collective self-consumption is electric mobility. Although the number of **Electric Vehicles** (**EVs**) is rising everywhere in the world (today more than 1 million EVs in the United States), there is still anxiety from buyers and prospects regarding the availability and locations of charging stations. Being able to charge electric vehicles easily and quickly at any time and in any place is going to be one of the most decisive factors in adopting new electric mobility.

Different initiatives have been launched to create trading platforms to allow people to charge at any station, private or public. Because there are currently 20,000 public charging stations in the US (almost 50 EV for one station), connecting EV's owners' private chargers would increase the network by hundreds of thousands. But to do so, these enterprises and individuals need to be paid accordingly for disposing of their chargers. This is where smart contracts come in as an important feature, to allow individuals and station owners to seamlessly trade and provide a secure experience for EV users.

Besides peer-to-peer trading and EV charging, which are the most advanced pilots, other use cases relying on blockchain can be thought of in the energy industry. For instance, a grid operator can use blockchain to optimize the supply in the network instead of shutting down a power station, which is a very expensive action, and manage electricity supply accordingly through the integration of demand response across the grid.

Big energy companies are starting to pay attention to opportunities offered by blockchain. Often, they are part of a consortium including banks, energy startups, or public authorities, where they provide business expertise and a specific need (a business case) and where the community brings technical knowledge or an integrated platform for answering needs. For instance, Shell and BP, as part of a broader consortium called Vakt Global, are now using a blockchain-based trading platform for crude oil, integrating smart contracts, which they hope will solve trade and settlement inefficiencies.

The decentralized pattern made possible by blockchain also incentivizes people and producers to trade capacity through a marketplace. A blockchain-enabled marketplace could trace and secure transactions between participants and keep private everyone's trading activity and data. Finally, the inherent security and transparency of the blockchain mean that it could have extensive applications across the power sector, from local microgrid projects to large-scale cross-border energy trading. A lot of issues need to be overcome in the energy sector to secure a sustainable system where energy generation, distribution, and consumption come together as a smart combination of clean resources, flexible markets, and cost-effective solutions.

Betting with blockchains

To conclude with smart contracts, let's consider the example of the tennis match between Federer and Nadal covered in `Chapter 2`, *A Technical Dive into Blockchain*.

The example dealt with the Betwin company as a middleman providing the truth and collecting bets. In fact, on a blockchain-based platform, we could use smart contracts to disintermediate the whole process by replacing Betwin with a code injected in the blockchain and run by every node of the network. The bettors would send money to the smart contract that would store the value and automatically repay the winner at the end of the match.

One typical realization of such a project is Cryptocup.io, which actually made it possible for betting to be automated, disintermediated, and self-organized. Cryptocup.io uses the Ethereum blockchain and smart contracts to enable individuals to place predictions on big soccer events such as the World Cup or Copa America.

Bets are very illustrative use cases to showcase smarts contracts. The Augur project understood this concept well enough to become a major reference in the blockchain ecosystem with its decentralized protocol that allows its users to build prediction markets. This technology is used to place and monitor bets from sports to stocks and from events to elections, in a global decentralized way and through smart contracts.

Digital identities

It is no secret that the world is evolving at a rapid pace. Never before have we witnessed so many changes happening in such a short period of time. Urbanization, as a matter of fact, has been accelerating these last fifteen years bringing important demographic and social changes.

Indeed, the population has continuously grown with an even more increasing proportion of the elderly. With 2030 just around the corner and 1960's baby-boomers, we'll reach a population of 8.5 billion people, among which 9% will be over 65 years old. Overpopulation combined with our modern over-consuming way of life has, unfortunately, a terrible impact on the environment. Climate change is a true concern and resource scarcity has been identified as a global trend by the World Economic Forum. But the most evident shift is the technological breakthroughs that impact every aspect of the global economy.

Corporations are spending more and more money in R&D (some of them almost 14% of their turnover) as they identified innovation being an important key growth driver. Technologies have invaded our everyday life, making it more connected and faster than ever before. Every industry has been impacted by new production cycles, by new ways of consuming, and by ubiquitous technologies and relentless communication between people, all of them triggered by disruptive innovations.

Due to these global shifts (urbanization, demographic changes, environmental issues, and technological progress), governments are trying to offset the negative consequences and make the most out of these changes to better handle citizenship, reinforce voting systems, and build smarter cities.

How can blockchains help with citizenship?

In the digital age, it is truly a hassle to keep track of what personal data has been handed over to which organization and what usage has been made out of it. Moreover, how can we ensure that this data is safely stored and cyber risks properly handled by third parties? Besides data sensitivity and personal information protection, there is also a major problem assessing someone digitally and managing their identities.

Indeed, how can someone prove that they are actually who they claim to be?

Such questions reach significant interest as dematerialization has become standard and ensuring proper authentication of the issuer and recipient has therefore hardened. Added to that, KYC and AML policies are gaining momentum as financial services endure tough digitization and need to comply against identity theft, tax fraud, and terrorism financing. Digital identity management has become a real matter and blockchain seems to bring an answer to that.

 A digital identity can be defined as a collection of information that represents a given individual in the digital world.

Control could be rendered to the users through blockchain, a challenge we often call **self-sovereign identity**. Instead of giving away information to access a service or an application, we could gain sovereignty by allowing only necessary data to be handed over, watching over which entity possesses which kind of knowledge about ourselves, and revoking access at any given time. Blockchain has the true potential to place the individual in control of their own data.

Experiments have been led mainly by international organizations such as the **United Nations** (**UN**), which set a goal to provide legal identities to the 1 billion human beings currently deprived of paper identity. This solution was suggested to counter the problem of the migrating population that the UN is helping through aid distribution. For their UN food programs that deliver every year 12 billion rations to 80 million people over the world, they developed a contactless card containing a photo and fingerprints that they captured for 15 million individuals. The main benefit of this solution resides in a large cost reduction induced by control procedures.

Another initiative worth mentioning is ID2020. It is a New-York based public-private partnership exploring blockchain to provide a permanent, shareable, and encrypted digital identity for individuals. Accenture and Microsoft joined the alliance to advance blockchain as a means to allow organizations to access certain personal data about refugees. The World Bank sustained the initiative and estimated the total cost of the project to reach $9 billion, among which $1 billion would be funded by the organization.

Best practices in identity management could be brought by India, which launched a program in 2010 called Aadhaar to provide every Indian resident a unique identifier linked to their biometric data and civil state. India, the second most populated country in the world, is currently helping the International Institute of Information Technologies based in Bangalore to develop the **Modular Open Source Identity Platform** (**MOSIP**) to build an infrastructure aiming to support a country-scale low-cost identification system. Lately, an agreement to implement this platform has been signed by Morocco, which will build a national blockchain-based registry to census the population.

Voting systems made easier with blockchains

How transparent and accurate are voting polls? How sensitive to fraud is the current voting system?

Every government in the world, along with the population, is concerned by these questions. Voting has always been a tricky topic for most democracies and it is not rare that, even in developed nations, we sometimes witness fraud or bribes during official elections (`https://www.irishtimes.com/news/politics/local-election-result-may-be-challenged-amid-electoral-fraud-allegations-1.3903639`). Also, the voting process can be harrowing and unclear, coupled with a required physical presence that often decreases the voting rate along with the fact that such methods are obsolete with numerous intermediaries and a high risk of corruption.

As of today, very few voting systems are performed online. Estonia is probably the most advanced e-democracy in the world, with a fifteen-year-old willingness to become the first 100% digital state. For the latest legislative election of March 2019, 44% of the voters made their choice online through Estonia's national voting system, called i-Voting.

While many countries such as the United States struggle to implement voting machines, Estonia has been a model of online voting infrastructure well recognized abroad. The first digital vote was performed in Estonia in 2005 but it became mainstream in 2011 thanks to a mobile application that electors could download with a special SIM card and a unique PIN code. Although the solution has been tested and secured over the years, several vulnerabilities have been identified by specialists as well as a fragility to scale-up if it was replicated in a bigger country.

Citizen participation and, more specifically, the voting system is a perfect example of what blockchain can help to upgrade. By implementing an easy-to-scale blockchain where each digital identifier would match a specific citizen, we could ensure that one person can vote securely, anonymously, and uniquely. And that would apply not only for big state decisions, but for any development that can be brought to the city (for example, a decision to construct the local football stadium submitted only to the citizens of the concerned neighborhood).

Moreover, with the inner incentivization model underlying blockchain, we could encourage citizens to participate in their civic life and reward their involvement with tokens usable to purchase specific services. Creating an immutable ledger of recorded votes would be a massive step forward in making elections more fair and democratic. Followmyvote, Voatz, and Democracy Earth are all projects trying to solve voting woes using blockchain to perform accurate identity management and online encrypted voting.

They have created voting platforms to bring transparency, convenience, and security to elections and polls of any kind. Voting systems are a prominent use case for blockchain although underlying political stakes dampen their practicality. When it comes to political power, disruption is often seen with mistrust and fear. Thanks to transparency and immutability, blockchain offers several options to boost voter participation and restore the public's trust in the electoral process and democracy.

Smart cities and public issues

Economic, social, technological, and political shifts are reshaping the world very quickly and new challenges arise for nations and particularly for cities. As governments are seeking to incorporate innovations within their cities, blockchain can offer something more.

According to the World Bank, more than 54% of the global population now lives in cities and contributes to more than half of the world's GDP. Because of this, cities are deeply concerned by global shifts set out previously: urbanization, demographic change, aging workforce, and environmental issues.

As a primary environment for a nation's development and wealth, cities must be able to embrace these changes to become a better place to live by becoming smarter, more collaborative, more inclusive, more sustainable, and more connected to provide enhanced services and a high quality of living for its citizens.

 Techopedia.com defines a smart city as being a city using technology to enhance the quality and performance of urban services as well as livability (https://www.techopedia.com/definition/31494/smart-city).

Smart cities allow operational efficiencies, maximize environmental sustainability efforts and create new services. Smart cities can become an enabler to counter downsides of urbanization and demographic explosion that impact the environment. Indeed, the ever-increasing population jeopardizes basic needs such as a clean habitat, water, energy, and infrastructure.

India launched, in 2015, its Smart Cities Mission, aiming to develop 100 smart cities in the country. This five-year program will cost $29.9 billion and is intended to promote sustainable and inclusive urban development that would match and secure the expected growth rate of India's cities. To make this happen, a lot of use cases have been thought of, from medical services to transportation; every city will have to improve its service and face urban challenges such as shortage of power, insufficient water supply, unaffordable cost of living, inadequate public transportation, and pollution.

Smart cities have to rethink the way they manage the ecosystem to provide better support and increase the quality of living. The internet has already brought many possibilities for cities to become more efficient, moving manual services to digital services and storing information paperless. Employment, healthcare, culture, transportation, environment, land management, or waste are fields where technology and innovation have an impact.

Several pilots have been conducted across the globe and can be cited as examples:

- The Myanmar government partnered with Telenor, one of the world's biggest phone operator, to overcome laborious birth and death recordings by launching a civil registration system in which is integrated a platform updated by several authorized parties.
- In general, the healthcare system is a very complex structure with lots of actors and sharp ethics issues; hence it is a field where innovation can trigger some changes and make considerable gains in time and effort. Remote patient monitoring with sensors can, as one example, detect blood and glucose levels in patients and send the resulting data to doctors for analysis and prognosis. Healthcare professionals can analyze all of the data collected by sensors to prescribe highly personalized treatments and medications for patients. One may even be able to 3D print their pill to take at home with no interference at all with their day-to-day routine. This example will soon be experienced in the new innovation-driven health hub currently being built in Dubai. Tons of medical services powered by AI or 3D printing will be provided to patients from all over the world.
- With a huge amount of data collected on citizens' movements and travels, the transportation system could be improved so that it would match the population needs in terms of routes and schedules. The Joint Transportation Management Center, based in New York (the largest transportation center in North America), is using hundreds of cameras, vehicle detectors, and advisory radios to manage congestion on expressways, predict incidents, strengthen on-the-spot intervention, and reduce delays.

Basically, new enablers and tools such as IoT, 3D printing, big data, connected devices, and wearables facilitate cities' transformation toward smarter cities. With blockchain now on the radar, cities can take their morphing one step further.

Think about it—in the three aforementioned pilots realized in Myanmar, Dubai, and New York, several common characteristics emerge:

- Data is shared between multiple parties.
- Data is updated by multiple parties.
- Data is centralized.
- There are requirements for verification.

These characteristics are typical criteria flagging the applicability of blockchain. Although the aforementioned use cases are very effective for a smart city, blockchain can be implemented to make them smarter. Indeed, it would bring decentralization, erase intermediaries, and above all, bring security among the systems and interoperability between them. Blockchain, in a smart city, acts as a secured, distributed, and decentralized database that multiple parties share transparently to ensure accuracy of information with no risk of alteration or clearance of the database. Also, blockchain can decrease the risk of systemic issues related to data security, inefficiency, lack of transparency, and corruption that will become more frequent in the digital age.

Blockchain potential has not yet been well-apprehended by governments when building smart cities although some of them have pioneered blockchain applications and proved how powerful, cost-effective, and efficient it is. Let's review some of them.

Improving healthcare systems with blockchains

We have already seen how Estonia has the best practice for e-democracy with its digital voting platform used to perform public elections securely and transparently. But voting has not been the only public mission to be disrupted in this 1.3 million inhabitant country. For Estonia, data integrity in medical records is critical and hospitals are confronted with a lack of secured platforms to store and share patient data, making them a primary target for hackers. Added to that, medical practitioners often have no insight into the patient's medical history, which makes providing appropriate healthcare solutions a painful process.

As an answer, the Estonian e-Health Foundation launched a project in 2016 aiming to use blockchain to secure and store all patients' health records and archive related activity logs. Estonia becomes the first country to implement blockchain for healthcare on a national scale enabling hospitals and doctors to safely store data like medical records and share with the authorized professionals the related information. This project, plugged into the already-digitized medical infrastructure called e-Health Record, improves data security as well as accuracy and speed diagnosis.

Can we achieve better administration with blockchains?

Governments and public organizations are often accused of being slow, opaque, and prone to corruption, not to mention their purportedly outdated methods for solving a problem that does not involve any digital approach. These statements are not entirely true, as many efforts have been undertaken in the past few years. Today, considering blockchain-based systems, governments and administration can significantly reduce bureaucracy and security inefficiency, as well as increase transparency throughout their operations.

Dubai, for example, is aiming to put its government documents on a blockchain by 2020 to help to assess, verify, and distribute welfare or unemployment benefits in a much more streamlined and secured way. The United Arab Emirates vice president announced that by 2021, 50% of the government's transaction will be achieved through a blockchain to save time and resources. The first step was taken by the Dubai Department of Finance, which recently launched a blockchain-powered payment system intending to provide a more accurate and transparent governance process, as well as to enable real-time payments within and between government structures.

Managing land with blockchains

In most developed countries, land management is handled through land registration systems that identify real properties and keep a record of past and current data regarding their ownership, value, and use. Because these land registries are managed by government institutions and because they have been built through a long and complex process, they often contain errors over ownership.

Even though digitization has accelerated the registration of real estate transactions, the time from purchasing a property to recording the sale can take up to 6 months. With blockchain, this time could be considerably reduced thanks to smart contracts that would automatically trigger and assert a transaction.

Also, with decentralized identity management provided by blockchain infrastructure, mistakes over ownership would not happen anymore. This project was undertaken by the Swedish land-ownership authority in 2016. After two years of testing, the authority has conducted a successful test between individuals to buy and sell properties through a specific blockchain.

They are now working on scaling this pilot to a national production although a more important problem still needs to be overcome: the Swedish law does not acknowledge digital signature as an authentic deed. This means that, until the Swedish regulators amend the current laws for citizens to be able to digitally sign a transaction, the project will not be supported.

How blockchains support employment and education

One notable feature of the employment system nowadays is that it is very shattered, with lots of actors and stakeholders. The problem is that there is a lack of confidence among job seekers and companies. The perfect match between them is often hard to carry out and headhunting and recruitment businesses have soared in the past decades.

Currently, HR firms have no way of knowing whether a prospective employee's resume is genuine or not. This issue regarding identity in the employment sector is a derivative from the original question: *how can someone prove they are who they claim to be?* Of course, there are diplomas and certifications to provide evidence for someone's curriculum, but that raises another question: *how trustworthy are these diplomas and certifications?*

Blockchain brings a solution to both problems. The first one would be overcome through interoperability (as demonstrated in the *Interoperability* section of this chapter) with the right to access official information submitted by official institutions on oneself. Information on a candidate's past experiences, skills and diplomas are inevitably possessed by the different institutions the candidate graduated from or worked for.

As a consequence, implementing a distributed and decentralized registry that allows the sharing of information upon the candidate's consent would erase the doubts regarding the veracity of their career and achievements. It is important to understand that, as regards GDPR regulations, such a claim registry would not store any personal information.

Instead, it would only store the public keys (the candidates' digital identities) to which are attached undisclosed rights to access one organization's database. Once the candidate has given full consent to access their past achievements, the recruiter is allowed to access personal information to the candidate's school, university, and previous employer databases to retrieve needed information. Actually, such a system would evidently answer the second question, certifying the authenticity of a diploma. But until then, there is a better solution to assert a diploma or certification with blockchain, specifically, hash functions. This takes us back to the *Authentication and trustworthiness* section of this chapter, where any given file could be hashed and sent in a transaction through a public blockchain, hence assessing the owner's identity of the original document.

Such a solution was developed by BCDiploma, a French startup that raised €1.2 million in May 2019 to promote EvidenZ, their Ethereum-based one-click certified data product.

Blockchains for waste management, charity, and others

Other use cases for making cities smarter with blockchain can be cited in this chapter but the list would be excessively long. For instance, we could go on illustrating the improvement of waste management, a challenge faced by most of the countries and cities worldwide and which is gaining significance. Blockchain could facilitate the tracking of waste the same way it does for some products in the commercial food industry (see the *Traceability* section of this chapter). Or more simply, it could provide an almost instantaneous payment system to engage people to sort garbage. Actually, this was made possible by the Plastic Bank, which compensates for plastic waste contribution from people with specific tokens usable in the Plastic Bank's partner shops.

We could also integrate, in this chapter, common complaints in the charity space related to embezzlement and misuse of collected funds. Endowments and charity show real inefficiencies and corruption, which sometimes prevent money from reaching those who were meant to receive it. Using blockchain to track donations erases every kind of fraud imaginable in this sector, ensuring that money will not end up anywhere but in the right wallet of the right charity. The Bitcoin-based charity, the Bitgive Foundation, is actually the first non-profit organization exploiting blockchain to provide a donation platform to track funds in real time, as well as share financial information on project results to donors.

Besides waste management and charity, smart cities could also gain efficiency through blockchain-based solutions in safety, mobility, entertainment, culture, and many other ranges of services. In fact, all of the use cases covered in this book could be listed in the list of challenges for a city to become smarter.

Financial securities and fundraising

Bitcoin is the first application that triggered the interest of blockchain, the first innovation allowing the transfer of digital value from peer-to-peer, the first cryptocurrency that disrupted the financial sector. By creating cryptographic money that's exchangeable between peers without trusted third parties, Bitcoin has gained the curiosity of those who see this new digital asset a threat to their core business model based on collecting fees upon money transfers as well as providing financial services to customers and enterprises.

Years have passed since Bitcoin came into existence, and today, cryptocurrencies are not the only blockchain-based applications out there that absolutely disrupt the financial sector.

After Bitcoin and cryptocurrencies, we witnessed the emergence of ICOs revolutionizing how funds were raised by entrepreneurs, another core business of the banks. Fundraising and financial services are activities usually reserved for certain economic actors such as venture capital funds, business angels, hedge funds, or asset management firms. But ICOs diverted these services by erasing frictions and bringing speed and transparency for both investors and entrepreneurs. Because ICOs do not provide equity shares like a traditional IPO, hence reducing the power of the investors and relationships with project leaders, we then witnessed the emergence of **Security Token Offerings** (**STOs**). Through STOs, a fraction of companies' capital is tokenized to increase liquidity and accessibility for individual investors. This process replaces the expensive and time-consuming traditional IPO to offer an affordable means to sell equity shares, threatening another core business for investment banks. Not every company can afford to go public, but STOs now enable, through the issuance of tokens, sales of financial instruments such as equity and debt.

With these new tools (cryptocurrencies, ICOs, and STOs) and more broadly with tokenization, actors of the financial sector have been very active in the past few years to raise awareness, explore the technology, and launch experimentations. Many fields in finance are being disrupted and, according to IHS Markit, a global information provider, most of the blockchain applications in production affect trade finance, cross border payments, change operations, and asset management. Projects using distributed ledger technologies such as blockchain in the financial sector will exceed $462 billion by 2030 (https://technology.ihs.com/610757/blockchain-in-finance-report-2019), a tremendous number explained by considerable gains from disintermediation.

As an example, in April 2019, a new platform was born to enable cash and cash equivalents issuers and investors to operate transactions on a short-term basis in a few minutes against two days usually. This platform called NowCP was created by several banks such as BNP Paribas and Natixis and the telecom company, Orange, to disrupt the short-term negotiable security market by bringing increased liquidity. The ultimate goal is to streamline treasury management for investors and issuers by extending range trading. Like any other blockchain-based project, NowCP will run in production once a sufficient number of stakeholders have joined the platform to achieve sufficient decentralization and, hence, robustness and security in transactions.

One other example worth mentioning to showcase the disruption of the financial sector is the recent news concerning the London Stock Exchange, which authorized, on April 17, 2019, the company 20|30 to run the first security token offering under the approval of UK's **Financial Conduct Authority** (**FCA**). The STO was conducted through a platform called TokenFactory where a pre-sale of 6 million security tokens were issued at £0.50 each on the London Stock Exchange. These tokens representing shares of 20|30's equity are based on smart contracts deployed on the Ethereum blockchain. This realization is an utmost application of what blockchain has already achieved in fundraising and capital markets. Note that it was mainly made possible, thanks to the proactive behavior of the FCA who was already providing sandboxes in 2017 for companies to experiment with projects without fear of being outlawed, a remarkable attitude for a public actor in the blockchain ecosystem. We shall underline that, although 20|30's STO is not the first STO ever, it is actually the first STO to be conducted by a stock exchange—in other words, by an official institution.

Many other initiatives have been led to allow companies to issue securities on a distributed ledger. Although it is preferable to operate under domestic financial authorities' agreement, some projects have been conducted through specific platforms built on purpose. A French company called Kriptown has brought equity fundraising to another level in its country. This platform has made tokenization the perfect tool to improve liquidity in the equity crowdfunding industry. Albeit crowdfunding experienced its finest hour in 2010, equity crowdfunding was still illegal in the US 3 years ago until the Jumpstart Our Business Startup Act (`https://www.sec.gov/spotlight/jobs-act.shtml`) (JOBS Act) came into effect.

With blockchain and tokenization, equity crowdfunding is witnessing a great advancement that will unlock a wider audience and larger liquidity, as well as greater interoperability and reinforced compliance. Kriptown's platform hosted its first STO for a startup called Tako (a car-sharing company) and succeeded in raising €475,000 in two months at the beginning of 2019. Concretely, Kriptown created a **special purpose vehicle** (**SPV**), which acquired shares of Tako's equity, which was then digitally represented on a blockchain—in other words, tokenized. Investors could purchase tokens representing a part of the SPV and could then be traded on a secondary market. This blockchain-based operation and tokenization provide many upsides. First, settlement periods, which usually take several weeks in private markets, are taken down to minutes. Second, KYC and AML procedures are much more facilitated as well as complying with European norms, which, as a consequence, allow large cost savings for the issuing company. Last, but not least, secondary markets operating under a common protocol now allow the transfer of tokens as easily as sending an email.

Other experimentations have been tested with blockchain in banks and insurances. These range from derivatives products where blockchain acts as a trade repository enabling regulators to know which assets are owned by whom at any time, to replacement of central agents responsible for ownership transfer such as updating registries of outstanding securities. Blockchain achieves fast and secured transactions as well as eases settlements meanwhile reducing costs and delays. Theoretically, blockchain and smart contracts can be used to facilitate every financial transaction. For example, dividend payment and coupon payment could be automated through smart contracts and stored in a single and trustless place through blockchain, although we are still waiting for a company to initiate such a project and still expecting regulatory bodies to address proper laws and policies to make these kinds of operation possible.

Digital uniqueness

The beginning of the 90s brought the internet as we know it today, a network in which computers can communicate using the TCP/IP protocol. Since the invention of the World Wide Web, the first internet-based application, computers have been able to exchange information endlessly across the network.

This mechanism, covered in `Chapter 5`, *An Economic and Historical Approach of Blockchain*, is called replication; the nodes (computers and servers) connected to the network (internet) can replicate the information to pass it on to the other nodes. Replication decreases the value of a digital item as it is transferred over the network. With Bitcoin, the world witnessed digital scarcity for the first time. This is how it works:

- First, an initial level of scarcity is induced by overcoming the double-spending problem, ensuring that a digital asset cannot be replicated when sent from one node to another.
- Second, Bitcoin's inherent algorithm creates a certain amount of token for each block validated until the total amount of tokens reaches 21 million. This means that, because no more, and no less than 21 million tokens will be issued in the end, Bitcoin will inevitably gain in value.

In this fashion, we can say that Bitcoin is deflationist money and a scarce digital resource as only a finite number of tokens are in circulation and none of them can be replicated between computers.

Another important characteristic to be mentioned about Bitcoin is that it is fungible, meaning that one Bitcoin is interchangeable with another Bitcoin. Fungibility is explained as being something of such nature that one part or quantity may be replaced by an equal part or quantity of the same nature. For instance, the euro and dollar are fungible money. Do you expect your bank to give you back the same bills and coins you deposited last year in your account? Probably not. Fungibility is an intrinsic characteristic of a currency: coins and bills cannot be individualized. Fungible things can be designated based on their nature (coins, milk, and gold) and their quantity (units, liters, and kilograms) and Bitcoin does not make an exception.

This characteristic is, however, a challenge to achieve true scarcity in the digital world. When it comes to artworks, diamonds, or buildings, which are not interchangeable and unique, it becomes different. These assets are not fungible; that is, each one is different from the other with its own trait. So, how can we manage non-fungibility in the digital world?

Crypto-collectibles

A new class of digital assets called crypto-collectibles has appeared lately as an answer to this issue. The most famous crypto-collectibles application is Cryptokitties, one of the world's first games to be built on blockchain (on Ethereum, actually). The concept is simple: you can buy kitties with Ether and breed them together to obtain an offspring out of it. You can then sell them, trade them, or buy other ones.

The principle behind it is that these kitties are unique and possessed by one and only one person. Therefore, each kitty represents a cryptoasset that is not interchangeable and has a value based on difficulty and the number of breeds needed to create it. The ambition of the founders was to prove through a simple game that digital uniqueness could be achieved thanks to blockchain, and that digital value can be transferred from one person to another securely and transparently, without the need of a central authority. This application was such a success that in December 2017 it was taking up too much available space for transactions to be processed by the Ethereum network and caused the pending transactions queue to witness a sixfold increase!

Uniqueness is a key feature in the digital world with many use cases to be thought of. Collectibles such as Cryptokitties are just the tip of the iceberg. Actually, any digital asset that is supposed to be unique can be traded and certified as one of a kind through a blockchain.

Non-fungible token standards

Uniqueness is made possible thanks to a specific kind of token where each token is different from the other. Most of the applications using non-fungibles tokens are developed on Ethereum because Ethereum makes available certain standards for developers to create a different kind of token according to the purpose of the application.

For example, the Ether token (the cryptocurrency) is based on a standard called ERC20 whereas the tokens underlying Cryptokitties have been developed according to the ERC721 standards, which include non-fungibility characteristics. ERC20 is the most popular standard used for the creation of tokens because they are fungible tokens that can be used as utilities or as money, which are the most common applications on Ethereum. ERC721, on the other hand, is the first standard enabling the creation of non-fungible tokens, with unique features.

This standard is very appropriate for several types of assets such as buildings, artworks, or specific financial products that are digitally reflected on Ethereum. It is particularly suitable for land registry management where ERC721 tokens represent a unique piece of land or a unique building. With physical assets represented as tokens, it is now possible for owners and investors to acquire almost instantaneously, securely, and in a cost-effective manner, a piece of land, artwork, or any unique valuable goods.

Card collection

Another prominent illustration of digital uniqueness challenges revolves around card collection. Have you ever collected Panini cards of your favorite players and teams, progressively sticking them in an album meant to be completed? With the internet, these paper-based collectibles were surely about to be replaced by digital ones. Unfortunately, as these images face a lack of fungibility, the internet struggled to deliver the same experience.

Hopefully, blockchain brought an answer to that. A project has gained popularity in the beginning of 2019 because it partnered with the most renowned football clubs such as Real Madrid or Arsenal to enhance the fan experience. This project, called Fantastec Swap is replicating in the digital world what Panini did in the 90s with their collectible cards. Fantastec is a blockchain-based digital collectibles platform that enables fans to discover, collect, and exchange official content such as players' bios, videos, or autographs from their favorite football team and players.

Because football is the most engaged sports of all and has an enormous fan base, challenges for clubs have shifted to convert fans into actual clients. By providing purchasable and tradeable player cards, Fantastec allows the clubs both to leverage their fan base to increase their flow-through ratio and foster engagement in general. Technically, Fantastec can be compared to Cryptokitties where kitties are replaced by real players. The difference resides in the degree of fungibility and uniqueness of certain player cards. Some are unique, others are not. All of the player cards have a certain degree of rarity, just like the old Panini cards.

This solution is one answer to many incredible challenges that the sports industry faces, especially around fan engagement where reputation and most of the money lie. Sports teams are trying desperately to gain insights about their fans to build lasting relationships. Most of the clubs know very precisely how many fans they have but only a few have a client base as large as their fan base. Applications like Fantastec, coupled with blockchain technology, can ensure a reliable growth driver as well as an innovative and fun way to engage more fans.

Tokenization of unique assets

In conclusion, after Bitcoin's demonstration of digital scarcity, a new layer has been implemented with non-fungible tokens, bringing uniqueness in a world where replication is usually the norm. The applications using non-fungible tokens attract new kinds of individuals and professionals, collectors, and niche consumers as well as players and investors.

As of today, very few applications allow trading of non-fungible assets to work in production because there is a strong legal and administrative framework to comply with. A unique painting can be digitally transcribed into an ERC721 token that will later be traded from one investor to another. However, as far as the law is concerned, the token will not be considered as the authentic certificate until the legal paper-based process has been completed.

That is why some professions such as notaries or auctioneers are not about to disappear, because there are still regulations about non-fungible assets where certifications, ownership and sale agreements must remain under the supervision of trusted third parties. And, as long as tokenization is not recognized by jurisdictions as a legal means to authenticate a unique painting's certificate, ERC721-based application will not become mainstream. In this context, it is still hard for blockchain entrepreneurs to advance decentralized digital asset management and link real-world items with so-called tokens.

Blockchain in the banking and finance sector

In the banking and finance sector, blockchain was first perceived as a threat when Bitcoin started to gain fame, supported by an active tech community, before realizing that some serious challenges could be advanced through this technology. Consequently, more and more projects were undertaken that led to an evolution of behaviors and spirits, turning the threat into an opportunity. Today, big actors are trying to get involved, sometimes successfully, sometimes for the sole marketing outgrowth, and sometimes for cautiously experimenting positive or negative outcomes.

As I am writing this chapter, other Fortune 500 companies are about to launch their own blockchain project. Nike is launching its cryptocurrency called Cryptokicks although we do not have much information yet about the project, which might focus on collectibles. Facebook officially announced, on June 18, 2019, the launch of the Libra project, expected to go live in 2020. We shall stop a moment to discuss this initiative since it was covered by multiple main media channels, a phenomenon that only happened when Bitcoin's price approached $20,000 at the end of 2017. Basically, the Libra will be a new cryptocurrency exchangeable across the world in a costless and almost instantaneous manner. Although Facebook is the initiator of the project, it will not be the only participant. As of the announcement, 26 other companies such as Spotify, Uber, Vodafone, Visa, and Coinbase have joined the movement and sit on the executive board of the Libra Foundation, a Switzerland-based entity legally bearing the project. All participants, including Facebook, will have equal rights in the management of the association. The Libra coin will take the form of a stablecoin, a coin backed by a real stock of assets like dollars, euros, or bonds. This means that the price of the Libra will not fluctuate according to supply and demand but rather the price of the basket on which it is based. To constitute this basket, each member agreed to bring $10 million to the Libra Foundation. Besides the cryptocurrency itself, the Libra Foundation plans to create a myriad of services and applications based on the Libra token. In other words, they will create an entirely new financial system in which Facebook will be able to become an independent financial structure, a kind of bank that offers financial services to its customers. And what better service provider than the company that knows you best? Only the future will tell whether this project is as revolutionary as it sounds, but, for now, Facebook is legitimizing cryptocurrencies and has taken a huge step forward in the ecosystem.

In any case, from regulation to arts, from banking to pharmaceuticals and from sports to cities, blockchain provides an innovative way to record and transfer value that is transparent, safe, auditable, and resistant to modifications. No architecture offers a better tamperproof and attack-resistant service than blockchain. Along with the different illustrations in this chapter, we showed how blockchain provides more transparency around the use and state of resources, more confidence in a trustless environment and a better representation of decision-making.

We are still in the very early stages of blockchain applications development. Due to blockchain's unripeness, enterprises struggle to reach a true implementation with a scaled, up-and-working application. As stated by Gartner in their 2018 Market Guide for Blockchain, most organizations are in the discovery phase as they are attempting to prove the viability of its use in their industry. Several experimentations have been initiated by large companies, some of them successfully turned into pilots, but very few eventually materialized into industrialized solutions. Hopefully, these challenges will be overcome in the coming years as the technology becomes more democratized and more accessible to a broad market. In fact, we can draw parallels with the internet's adoption curve, an innovation that strived to demonstrate its usefulness in the 80s, experimented by large telecom and technology firms before being massively adopted worldwide. The following is a screenshot from `https://www.internetworldstats.com/emarketing.htm`, showing the internet's adoption curve in the percentage of the world population:

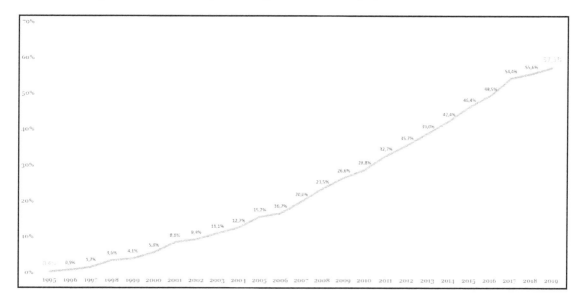

Now that we've reached the end of this chapter, you should be able to capture the business issues that blockchain solves. You should also have a clear understanding that blockchain is not a cure for any woe but, instead, brings trust in a decentralized environment, increases reliability between stakeholders, reduces cost through disintermediation, and achieves mass coordination through decentralization.

In conclusion, we shall state that like any other disruptive technology, the democratization of blockchain is slowed and challenged by cultural change where blockchain is often confused with Bitcoin or cryptocurrencies. The absence of standardization increases apprehension in the ecosystem which is often assimilated as an underworld exploited for illicit activities and criminals. A large misunderstanding and the complexness of the technology frighten decision-makers and business executives who are reluctant to experiment with certain developments in their respective industries.

Summary

Throughout this chapter, we've demonstrated how traceability and transparency can be fulfilled collaboratively, securing and enhancing the supply chain and asset maintenance in industrial sectors. We also demonstrated how processes can be improved in healthcare and food, how interoperability enhanced security between connected devices, and how undisclosed information could be shared in a competitive environment seamlessly and protectively.

You've learned how blockchain brings a robust authentication on a network to decrease counterfeit and forgery, mainly in the luxury goods industry and in arts. Also, we showed how blockchain enables new business opportunities between competitors, just like in the automotive and commercial food industries.

We also demonstrated, through the different sections, that financial inclusion increased in emerging markets as financial services on the blockchain gain critical mass and that financial organizations were about to be disintermediated as new services and value exchanges are created directly on the blockchain. Finally, we demonstrated that assets trading was facilitated as all kinds of value exchange can be hosted on the blockchain, and that tokenization enhanced tradability, thanks to increased liquidity.

In the next chapter, we will have a look at how blockchain is likely to be apprehended in the future and how the ecosystem will handle the fast changes the technology is bringing to the business world.

8
Future Outlook for Blockchain

So far, we have covered fundamental, technical, economic, and social concepts around blockchain, as well as provided definitions and legal information around cryptocurrencies and tokens. We also have illustrated several applications that were implemented in the business world. As a decision maker, you hopefully have enough elements to build a personal opinion about the technology and figure out how relevant it is for your business.

Blockchain is currently on the verge of becoming the next big technology. Between 2009 and 2014, the ecosystem was struggling to reach a certain level of adoption to make Bitcoin a reliable decentralized digital currency. Enthusiasts were focusing on trading activities, slowly discovering the underlying technology and its disintermediated and transparent features. The birth of Ethereum changed many things, fostering a stronger commitment from developers and entrepreneurs. New tools emerged such as smart contracts and more lately the Lightning Network. Democratization surged when cryptocurrencies gained worldwide media coverage spearheaded by Bitcoin's price rise, making emulation within the financial realm. **Initial coin offerings** (**ICOs**) soared and many blockchain start-ups have seen the light of day with several projects successful enough to compete with the world's most valuable start-ups.

The previous chapters were intended to help you picture the mechanics of a blockchain, the political background, and the different applications made across industries and countries to solve business inefficiencies such as interoperability, data reliability, and security. In this chapter, we are now going to cover key insights about a possible future based on changes that have already occurred and others that will most likely happen to situate blockchain on the technological route toward a redesigned and reshaped global economy. Being able to understand the development of the technology in the coming years is important for decision makers to grasp blockchain's potential in bringing remarkable business opportunities as well as enabling growth in the digital age.

In this chapter, we will discuss the following topics:

- Accretive investments
- The next GAFA
- A plausible shift for governments
- Threats

Increasing investment in blockchain

Usually, one indicator that economists like to quote to underline the expansion of an innovation is the amount of investment made over a certain period. As of June 2019, the total market capitalization of all cryptocurrencies was $320 billion (`https://coinmarketcap.com/fr/charts/`) and more than 1,200 projects were financed through ICOs for a total amount of $7.8 billion in 2018 (`https://www.icodata.io/stats/2018`).

In comparison, global venture capital funding reached $250 billion (`https://assets.kpmg/content/dam/kpmg/xx/pdf/2019/01/kpmg-venture-pulse-q4-2018.pdf`) that same year, of which more than $4 billion was allocated to blockchain start-ups. That is, 1.6% of the total venture capital funding was dedicated to blockchain start-ups, a fourfold increase compared to 2017, where they had raised a total of $1 billion.

2017 was actually the year where venture capital fundraising was outperformed by ICO fundraising, which meant a huge spike in popularity among project leaders (and scammers!). ICO fundraising for that sole year exceeded $5.4 billion (`https://www.cbinsights.com/research/blockchain-vc-ico-funding/`), an enormous amount considering the newness of the method and the financial risks associated with it.

These facts show that there is a shift in the venture capital funding model, where traditional **venture capital** (**VC**) funds are being replaced by specialized investment vehicles targeting blockchain businesses. That is, more and more VC is focused on building portfolios and know-how around blockchain.

Successful blockchain businesses

Digital Currency Group, founded in 2015, and Blockchain Capital, founded in 2013, are the biggest players in the sector, having respectively closed 127 and 57 deals since their creation. They contributed to the blockchain start-up funding upswing in 2017 and transformed several projects into successful financial investments for their backers. Coinbase is probably the most illustrative example of such accomplishment: created in 2012, they raised $108 million in August 2017, followed by a $300 million funding round in October 2018, which brought their valuation to $8 billion. It is a massive number for a cryptocurrency storage and trading platform, but, most of all, an impressive valuation for a six-year-old start-up. As of 2019, only DoorDash, Stripe, Airbnb, Juul, WeWork, and Uber have done better in this timeframe. The following screenshot displays the home page of Coinbase:

Coinbase was founded in 2012 by Brian Armstrong and Fred Ehrsam as an online platform to purchase Bitcoin through wire transfer. In 2014, they already had 1 million users and three years later received a license from the New York State Department of Financial Services to widen their offer. As of August 2018, Coinbase claims 20 million users worldwide.

Along the same lines, Binance is a two-year-old start-up that has become one of the world's biggest exchanges in 2018, in terms of volume traded ($2 billion every day as of June 2019 according to `coinmarketcap.com`). In order to deliver their crypto-to-crypto exchange platform providing buying and selling services, they raised $15 million through an ICO in July 2017, which they completed two months later with a $10 million VC-backed fundraising round.

As of June 2019, Binance has made so many achievements that the market capitalization of their underlying token **Binance Coin** (**BNB**) is now hitting $4 billion. Although that number cannot be considered as the value of the company, it clearly highlights its attractiveness to investors and clients, especially since the start-up successfully created an array of additional services such as Binance Launchpad, a platform to facilitate the launch of ICOs, and Binance Labs, both an investment fund and incubator.

 BNB was created by Binance to incentivize its users by providing means to pay exchange fees. The $4 billion valuation is the valuation of the total issued BNB tokens. The token soared from $10 cents during the ICO conducted in July 2017 to $32 two years later.

ICOs and VC funding in blockchain start-ups are still a drop in the capital-raising ocean, but the trend is moving upward as more and more companies gain interest in the technology. IBM, who are considered today's most advanced enterprise in the ecosystem, has invested more than $200 million (`https://www.mckinsey.com/industries/financial-services/our-insights/blockchains-occam-problem`) in developing blockchain-based solutions.

Google, which has surprisingly remained discreet about its actions, has already invested in six different projects and partnered with blockchain platforms, although no official announcement has ever been made by the web giant. Truth be told, the biggest investors in the ecosystem are banks. Bank of China, J.P.Morgan, Bank of America, and Wells Fargo are part of the top 10 biggest public companies (`https://www.forbes.com/sites/michaeldelcastillo/2018/07/03/big-blockchain-the-50-largest-public-companies-exploring-blockchain/#4e02c5482b5b`) that are experimenting with blockchain, either by investing directly in start-ups or by buying over-the-counter products.

Blockchain and cryptocurrency investment trends

Investments in blockchain have soared to billions in just a matter of months. Note that we are talking about investments in blockchain, not in cryptocurrencies. The crypto bubble, which burst in late 2017, is sometimes compared to the dot-com bubble of 2000. In fact, it is important to highlight the difference between the tokens subject to speculation and the financial health of the companies supporting them. The large investments made by individuals and asset management firms in cryptocurrencies do not tie them to the effective success (or failure) of the company that issued them.

For instance, Binance's performance is not supposed to be correlated to the performance of their token (BNB) since they are not actual shares of Binance's capital. As a decision maker, you should remain cautious by accurately differentiating investment trends on cryptocurrencies and blockchain projects even though the two provide a somewhat good representation of the market perception of the technology.

The next GAFA

It's been a few years since Google, Apple, Facebook, and Amazon (often nicknamed GAFA) have shared the leaderboard as the most valuable companies in the world.

In the coming years, there is a possibility that GAFA's market capitalization will be outperformed by blockchain-based tokens. We witnessed Bitcoin's market capitalization reach $320 billion in December 2017, and it is not so far-fetched to imagine new growth bringing either this cryptocurrency or another promising one such as Ether to the $1.5 trillion threshold that GAFA struggle to reach.

The future of cryptocurrencies

Precautions must be taken, however, because these tokens will not represent an outstanding share but a number of how much an individual is willing to pay to access the product or service. That is, if Ethereum's market capitalization reached $1.5 trillion in the coming years, that would mean that the number of Ether multiplied by their market price returns the total market capitalization of the cryptocurrency, which is the total amount paid to possess Ether.

This number would not represent the value of the Ethereum Foundation or any entity related to Ethereum, not only because foundations and associations are nonprofit organizations, but mainly because no entity actually backs the cryptocurrency Ether, which is totally independent and free from governing bodies. However, it is interesting to note that the most valuable companies in the world will probably be surpassed by blockchain-based tokens in terms of market capitalization, meaning that you would find it more valuable to hold Ether or Bitcoin than an actual share of Google, Apple, Facebook, or Amazon.

Decentralized enterprise takeover

Another possible scenario is that original internet-native enterprises may be replaced by blockchain-native ones. Several projects are attempting to transform proven business models in a decentralized manner, to increase reliability and transparency. For example, Presearch is a community-empowered search engine that incentivizes people by providing tokens for every usage of the product. Their ultimate goal is to display contents and searches according to the community's interests and in respect of fair and transparent rankings. This business model was built to tackle Google's monopoly, which has become the primary gatekeeper to the internet and its underlying power to shape perceptions.

OpenBazaar and Particl are both promising start-ups currently disrupting Amazon's business model by enabling individuals to exchange physical goods from all over the world. These blockchain-based marketplaces rely on an escrow system where each peer has interest in properly providing the service and payment to the other peer, all of this in a trustless ecosystem where no central entity levies transaction fees for ensuring correct transfer of goods.

Since 2016, social media platforms such as Facebook, YouTube, and Instagram have a new competitor: Steemit, a decentralized and censorship-resistant social media platform that rewards its users with tokens for publishing and curating content. With growing anxiety about information manipulation on traditional social media platforms, the need for a censorship-resistant network is gaining attention, and Steemit seems to overcome these serious issues by providing an efficient infrastructure for personal data ownership and content monetization.

It would be a hasty judgement to say that Presearch, OpenBazaar, and Steemit could respectively replace Google, Amazon, and Facebook in the future. As of June 2019, their influence in the ecosystem cannot even be compared to GAFA's influence on economic and social behaviors. But still, these blockchain-native companies present a totally different business model, prioritizing customer interests above profitability, mass coordination above unilateral decision making, and transparency above opacity: a business model that fits with a collaborative economy that might one day become a substitute for the traditional capitalistic operating models.

A plausible shift for governments

Since Facebook's announcement of the Libra project in June 2019, it is most likely that developed nations will create some kind of a digital currency. Do not get confused, a cryptocurrency is a digital currency, but a digital currency is not necessarily a cryptocurrency.

On the scale of a country, the choice of a centralized or decentralized digital currency will depend on the infrastructure and governance on which it is based. Nations witnessing unstable economies and relying on weak institutions will probably be the first to experiment and explore decentralized digital currencies stimulated by political concerns rather than technological ones. Decentralized digital currencies (cryptocurrencies) can become a powerful tool to overcome monetary challenges.

Just like Facebook, countries will enter the ecosystem through the cryptocurrency's front door before exploring more opportunities. In the coming years, countries will compete with each other to become a digital-first nation, supporting the best innovative projects.

> *"A crypto-nation could be defined as a country encouraging blockchain initiatives, embracing cryptocurrencies and working toward a conducive regulatory framework."*

Becoming a crypto-nation is a long process and some countries are more inclined to undertake that process than others. For example, Australia, the United Kingdom, and Singapore have adopted a positive attitude, undertaking projects and initiating action upon cryptocurrencies, regulation, and infrastructure.

On the other hand, countries such as China and Bolivia have forbidden the sale and purchase of cryptocurrencies in their territory since 2014, as shown in the following diagram:

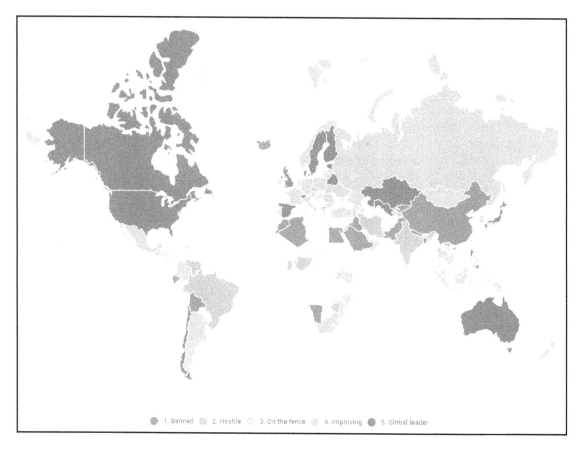

The preceding diagram is an overview of each country's perception toward cryptocurrencies.

Threats and risks in the ecosystem

Despite the tremendous amounts spent to experiment with blockchain, few proof of concepts have been turned into pilots and even fewer into industrialized solutions. These many failures have left some people skeptical and assuming that the technology is not suitable for broad market applicability, as it only answers specific needs.

Most critics deplore the use of blockchain solely for marketing purposes, increasing the value of a brand by showing shareholders and customers the firm's ability to innovate. Misjudged expenses, difficulty-to-estimate profitability, and the impeding of stable revenue streams are also arguments pointed out by detractors, as well as the complications in developing scaled-up solutions.

Lots of technical challenges such as scalability and user-friendliness still have to be overcome as the technology gains popularity, and as bigger networks are formed. Due to the cryptocurrency bubble bursting in 2017, blockchain suffered a sharp fall into a valley of disillusionment, especially because of the bear market that prevailed afterward. The upside was that the developer community seized the declining media coverage as an opportunity to push the technology further. Unfortunately, new innovations were also surfacing in the meantime, and one of them, known as quantum computing, could actually jeopardize blockchain's usefulness.

As a decision maker, you must be aware that this emerging technology threatens blockchain by solving certain problems exponentially faster than any traditional computer. Microsoft defines it as the following:

> *"Operating with nanoscale components at temperatures colder than intergalactic space, quantum computing has the potential to solve some of the world's toughest challenges. It takes only days or hours to solve problems that would take billions of years using today's computers."*

Classical computers store information as parts that hold a single binary value (1 or 0), whereas quantum computers store information as qubits, which can hold both values (1 and 0) at the same time, allowing vast numbers of calculations simultaneously.

So, how is that a threat to blockchain?

Well, the blockchain is said to be practically unhackable due to the combination of consensus mechanisms and algorithms that require tremendous computing power to add and chain the data in the ledger (since blockchains rely on proof-of-work protocols). And, it requires even more computing power to modify data when it was already validated by the network.

In this fashion, the industrialization of quantum computing, which makes any mathematical problem a mere formality, would definitely render blockchain obsolete. Altering a 20-times confirmed transaction (winding back 19 blocks in the past, which is said to be impossible with today's computers) would require a fraction of a second because re-computing all subsequent hashes would become a piece of cake for quantum computers.

Although this emerging technology is likely more than a decade away, some well-known manufacturers have taken incremental steps along the way. On January 16, 2019, IBM released a commercially ready version of a quantum computer called Q System One, a nine-by-nine feet glass-protected machine (`https://newsroom.ibm.com/2019-01-08-IBM-Unveils-Worlds-First-Integrated-Quantum-Computing-System-for-Commercial-Use#assets_115:1612`). Although the industrialization and miniaturization of quantum computers will not happen in the very near future, IBM's latest announcement is more than relevant as it can compromise the fundamental characteristics of blockchain.

Summary

As we saw in this chapter, in the coming years, it is most likely that blockchain will gain more and more consideration, hopefully gaining in maturity and recognition from governments and business leaders. Promising use cases will continue to emerge, eventually turning more and more into industrialized and user-friendly solutions. We also saw that funding will rise in importance, mostly thanks to new financing methods such as **security token offerings** (**STOs**), bringing the tokenization of financial securities to the next level. In contrast, we highlighted the emerging technologies such as quantum computing that could threaten blockchains supported by proof-of-work mechanisms, and other threats such as scalability and speed, which could handicap proper development of the technology.

In the next chapter, we will explain why we sometimes talk about a private, semi-private, or public blockchain. We will also focus on the evolution of blockchain with a technical scope and discover some infrastructures and cloud-based solutions.

3
Section 3: Blockchain for Business Leaders

As a manager in your organization, what are the inherent ingredients to take into consideration regarding your functional expertise and industry? After reading this part, you should be able to understand how blockchain can help you to solve business challenges and improve processes within your organization. As a decision maker, you should be able to understand whether a blockchain is useful for your business issues and be able to select a suitable framework to implement.

This section comprises of the following chapters:

- Chapter 9, *Infrastructures and Cloud-Based Solutions*
- Chapter 10, *Defining Your Needs*

Infrastructures and Cloud-Based Solutions

9

In this chapter, we will cover some of the most interesting blockchain infrastructures available today for developing a blockchain-based application or launching a blockchain-based project. The Bitcoin and Ethereum blockchains are not unique. Some infrastructures have appeared in the past few years, enabling fresh functionalities, such as setting conditions, defining a certain level of privacy within the network, or certifying nodes. In this chapter, we will explore some of these enterprise-grade solutions, namely Quorum, Hyperledger, Aergo, and Corda, and explore cloud-based solutions such as the IBM Blockchain Platform and Oracle Blockchain Platform, which we already mentioned in previous chapters. Here, we will also explore other **Blockchain-as-a-Service** (**BaaS**) providers such as **Amazon Web Services** (**AWS**) and Microsoft Azure and explore in slightly greater depth what services they offer and how effective they are.

In this chapter, we will cover the following topics:

- The evolution of blockchains
- Private, semi-private, and public blockchains
- J.P. Morgan's Quorum
- Hyperledger
- Aergo
- Corda
- Microsoft Azure
- AWS
- IBM
- Oracle
- Key takeaway

The evolution of blockchains

First, it is important to underline that there are several generations of blockchain on the market. The Bitcoin blockchain is considered the first generation, a very secure and decentralized infrastructure, which is why more and more miners are joining the network, but with low performance in terms of processing transactions and weak upgradability; in other words, users cannot do much more with Bitcoin's blockchain than send Bitcoin. Ethereum is considered the second generation of blockchain because it implemented major improvements to the initial protocol such as smart contracts. The third and fourth generations of blockchain are mostly focused on increasing the number of transactions per second, as well as providing enterprises with a flexible and suitable infrastructure for their needs. Aergo, Quorum, and Hyperledger can be cited as examples of these new blockchains; they set out to help the technology evolve dramatically by enhancing reliability and overcoming technical difficulties while increasing scalability. The following diagram shows the various generations of blockchain:

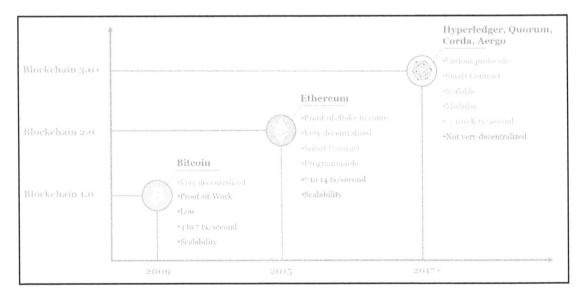

Private, semi-private, and public blockchains

Secondly, you must be aware that blockchains can take three different forms: public, private, or semi-private. Bitcoin and Ethereum are both public blockchains (also called permissionless blockchains), meaning that there is no restriction on who can become a node, who can use the service, and who can validate the transactions. They both benefit from a high degree of decentralization and do not require a supervisory body as the infrastructure, and their governance are self-organized. On the other hand, private and semi-private blockchains (also called permissioned blockchains) have a smaller degree of decentralization because only authenticated stakeholders can join the infrastructure. Therefore, they have a reduced number of nodes and miners compared to public blockchains. Their governance can be partially decentralized (we call such an organization a consortium) or totally centralized. In that case, roles are predefined for each member and transactions are validated and recorded on a private registry that only identified parties can read. To some extent, the term private blockchain (or permissioned blockchain) is a malapropism for designating a distributed ledger technology.

As a decision maker, you must remain careful with the terminology employed for private blockchains and the way they are implemented. Once again, keep in mind that a blockchain is an IT infrastructure that allows digital values to flow securely and transparently in a decentralized ecosystem without the need for a trusted third party. As soon as there is trust in an ecosystem, you can assume that blockchain is not relevant. Some so-called private blockchains only assemble actors that already trust each other: what is the point of having a protocol for recording transactions in a consensual manner when you know that there are no interest in skewing the data? A distributed ledger would suffice.

So, why bother implementing private blockchains? Well, they seem to provide better answers for enterprise-level issues, compared to public blockchains, that are condition-free, transparent, and pseudonymous. And actually, some projects have shown real applications. In fact, permissioned blockchains can be very useful for a group of stakeholders to handle a business process in common. They know each other but they don't trust one another.

To achieve high performance, scalability, and security in a private or semi-private network, some features had to be adapted within the infrastructure. Consensus protocols used in closed organizations differ from those used by Bitcoin or Ethereum (proof-of-work) because the nodes validating the transactions do not need to compete based on computational power. Instead, they compete based on their reputation within the network (proof-of-authority) or based on a voting system (delegated proof-of-stake). In any case, whatever consensus protocol is chosen for a blockchain, it should be Byzantine Fault-Tolerant, meaning that it should enable a distributed system to reach consensus (that is, an agreement on the same value) even when some nodes of the network are faulty. In other words, it should be able to overcome the problem illustrated by Byzantine General Problems (see Chapter 2, *A Technical Dive into Blockchain*). Proof-of-work, proof-of-stake, proof-of-authority, and delegated proof-of-stake are all Byzantine Fault-Tolerant protocols used according to the extent of decentralization needed, the permissions that need to be granted to some nodes to perform actions on the network, data velocity, and scalability. Most permissioned blockchains rely on voting and lottery-based consensus such as proof-of-stake and delegated proof-of-stake.

This latter is an alternative version of the proof-of-stake protocol, which, as a reminder, elects a miner based on the number of tokens (or stake) they possess. Delegated proof-of-stake is often compared to a technological democracy because it combines real-time voting and reputation to achieve consensus. Every token-holder can vote to elect a validator that eventually earns enough votes to become a delegate. After becoming a delegate, the node can then validate the transactions and collect the rewards for doing so. If they misbehave, voters can withdraw their votes to *fire* the bad actor from validating and securing the network. Also, the voting power of a token holder (known as the voting weight) is determined by how many tokens the account is holding. This protocol benefits from a high degree of decentralization and enables a fast process for validating the transactions. On the other hand, the bigger the network, the slower it becomes as the voting process increases latency. Delegated proof-of-stake hence includes a trade-off between decentralization and scalability.

Regarding scalability, proof-of-authority is a better alternative. It is an efficient protocol for permissioned blockchains that was proposed in 2017 by the co-founder of Ethereum, Gavin Wood. This protocol arbitrarily identifies nodes that will validate transactions. These nodes are chosen based on their reputation to become trustworthy entities that will have the responsibility for validating and securing transactions. To become a node within a blockchain relying on proof-of -authority, a user has to undergo a tough identification process, linking their digital identity to their real one and disclosing personal information that prevents wrongdoings. The fact that proof-of-authority includes only a restricted number of nodes allows the infrastructure to validate more transactions (that is, increase the block size) and lower the transaction fees to zero. Because the nodes are identified, they are incentivized based on their reputation and not on an underlying token, which explains why most blockchains based on proof-of-authority do not have a cryptocurrency. This kind of consensus is favored mostly in private blockchains such as Quorum, which was developed by J.P. Morgan, who took inspiration from proof-of-authority for its consensus algorithm.

Now that we have seen the different types of blockchain and why their features vary according to the needs, we will explore some famous infrastructures that were built to face enterprise-grade challenges.

J.P. Morgan's Quorum

Quorum was conceived by J.P. Morgan, the world's biggest bank in terms of market capitalization, and is basically a private version of Ethereum, open source and supported by Ethereum's community. Quorum uses a management of confidentiality that Ethereum does not offer, enabling participants to decide whether their transactions should remain private or be displayed publicly. Quorum also integrates enhanced transactions and contract privacy, as well as better performance in general. Quorum has great potential to be massively adopted by banking actors and financial institutions to the point that J.P. Morgan is willing to manage this activity separately from its banking activity. J.P. Morgan is also the first bank to deploy its own cryptocurrency, JPMCoin, a Quorum-based currency indexed on the US dollar that digitally represents money transfers between institutional actors, investors, and banks.

Another application made from Quorum is Vakt (see `Chapter 7`, *Blockchain for the Business World and Achievements*). This energy commodity trading platform aims to build a digital ecosystem to facilitate and enhance the oil business worldwide. Vakt takes the form of a consortium that has created a transaction platform as a single source of truth for the trade life cycle. Based on Quorum, BP, Shell, and Total now benefit from peer collaboration to combine market expertise and enhance the way issues are addressed, as well as increased speed and security of transactions in the industry.

Quorum was built mostly to answer specific needs in the financial industry, but it can actually be ported to similar sectors facing similar issues, such as avoiding exposure of financial transactions (that is, it can erase the pseudonymity underlying most public blockchains), increasing the speed of financial settlements, and retaining control of participants' identities (that is, preventing malicious parties from joining the network). Quorum's purpose is very specific but it is not the only permissioned blockchain trying to improve how certain industries operate.

Hyperledger

Hyperledger is a project that is gaining the most attention in the ecosystem and it is important that, as a decision maker, you gain awareness of it. As many blockchains are built from scratch for lots of different needs all over the world, the Hyperledger Project, launched by the Linux Foundation, is trying to standardize and democratize blockchain within the business world. Instead of letting companies solve their issues on their own, Hyperledger combines cross-industry knowledge and a modular approach to allow enterprises to build customized blockchains.

In 2015, the Linux Foundation, the nonprofit organization enabling mass innovation through open source, announced the collaboration of industry leaders to advance blockchain technology at an enterprise level. The original goal was—*to develop an open source distributed ledger framework to build robust, industry-specific applications, platforms, and hardware systems to support business transactions*. This is how the Hyperledger project was born.

The first members to join the movement were mostly banks, financial services firms, or IT companies. But as time went by, more and more corporations joined the project to the point that the member list, as of September 26, 2018, reached 270 contributing organizations from very different sectors and horizons. We can find in that list big industry-leading firms as well as startups, from logistics to healthcare and from finance to government, all of them having contributed either financially or by providing lines of code and development progress. As of June 2019, Hyperledger hosts 13 projects with more than 11 million lines of code and close to 28,000 participants who have come to 110+ meetups around the world.

"Distributed ledgers are poised to transform a wide range of industries."

- Jim Zemlin, Executive Director of the Linux Foundation,
after the launch of the Hyperledger Project in 2015

As blockchain is a recent innovation and a hard-to-catch concept for non-tech profiles, the need for cross-industry collaboration widened and Hyperledger appeared as a remedy.

 You have to understand that Hyperledger is not a company, not a cryptocurrency, and not a blockchain. It is a worldwide collaborative effort to transparently and openly enlighten others on blockchain's potential to solve business issues.

Hyperledger wrote a charter at the beginning of 2016, a kind of whitepaper stating its guidelines and what it is trying to achieve. Among the four missions announced, we can read the following:

- Create an enterprise-grade, open source, distributed ledger framework and codebase
- Promote participation of leading members of the ecosystem

What you have to remember about this charter is that the Linux Foundation, through its Hyperledger Project, is creating an environment in which communities of software developers and companies meet and coordinate to build blockchain frameworks. Hence, it is an open source organization in which you can find ongoing blockchain-related projects. All of them are non-currency projects and industrial applications. And that's an important point. You won't have any Hyperledger coin issued because the project doesn't intend to host its own cryptocurrency like Ethereum, for example.

"By not pushing a currency, we avoid so many of the political challenges of having to maintain a globally consistent currency."

- Brian Behlendorf, Hyperledger Executive Director

In summary, Hyperledger is a global movement, organized in several projects, initiated by the Linux Foundation, led by renowned people from the tech, open source, and data fields with years of experience and supported by 270 contributing companies and organizations aiming to develop non-currency blockchain-based projects for the business world. Let's explore what services are provided.

Hyperledger Sawtooth

Hyperledger Sawtooth is one of two projects currently available and production-ready.

Hyperledger Sawtooth is a blockchain mainly developed by Intel that intends to test the functionality of a new consensus mechanism called **Proof of Elapsed Time** (**PoeT**) and to allow an enterprise to run distributed ledgers maintained without a central authority.

PoeT is an algorithm that attempts to distribute network mining rights through a fair random system. It aims to eliminate environmental and energy-consumption issues underlying the proof-of-work consensus algorithm used by Bitcoin and other cryptocurrencies. The process follows a fair lottery system instead of rewarding the most powerful node. In short, each participating node in the network is required to wait for a randomly chosen period of time, and the first one to complete the designated waiting time is designated to validate the transactions.

In their presentation video, Hyperledger illustrates the potential of Sawtooth with the seafood supply chain, where Sawtooth provides an immutable record of provenance and the lineage of various goods such as fish. Thanks to the Internet of Things (physically connected devices) and sensors combined with Sawtooth, it is possible to trace any fish's journey from ocean to table. Sawtooth was written in Python and its target is to provide blockchains that could eventually be applied to the Internet of Things and various financial systems.

Hyperledger Fabric

Hyperledger Fabric is the second currently available and production-ready project, driven under the mentoring of IBM. As of June 2019, Fabric is the most widely-adopted blockchain by the biggest enterprises, providing a base on which to build a specific blockchain for specific industries and run applications that are related to specific needs.

It's not beginner-friendly at all, but it deserves credit for providing design and customization to meet precise requirements. Built as a modular framework where applications can easily scale up to any level, Fabric intends to provide basic blockchain features such as transparency, decentralization, and security.

Hyperledger Burrow, Indy, and Besu

Beside Sawtooth and Fabric, the following are other projects worth mentioning:

- Hyperledger Burrow is a permissionable smart contract machine developed to the specification of the **Ethereum Virtual Machine** (**EVM**).
- Hyperledger Indy is a distributed ledger built for decentralized identities. It provides tools, libraries, and reusable components for creating and using independent digital identities. It doesn't use proof-of-work and uses blockchain-based identity solutions.
- Hyperledger Iroha is a blockchain framework designed to be simple and easy to incorporate into infrastructure projects that require distributed ledger technology.

Let's put Burrow and Indy in perspective with a use case presented in the Hyperledger whitepaper.

Usually, banks gather **personally identifiable information** (**PII**) on every customer and prospect to assess a risk if a loan is requested. This information is sensitive and a juicy target for hackers. Moreover, loan applicants often need to share these information with several banks to increase their chance of obtaining a loan while also increasing the chance of this information being abused. With Hyperledger Indy, applicants can share only the information the banks need to make a decision without placing any personal data in the equation. Thanks to a secured blockchain, applicants can disclose the assessed information confidently and banks can conform with regulations and rely on this distributed ledger that acts as a source of truth. On top of that, the Hyperledger Burrow system turns the loan application into a smart contract, attaching identities to the loan.

Hyperledger Besu is the latest project to join Hyperledger and the first software in the community to be operable on a public blockchain, Ethereum. Emerging as a solution built jointly with ConsenSys, Besu offers a large modularity to build business applications on a public or a private network. This project was unsurprisingly released in August 2019, less than a year after Hyperledger announced a strategic partnership with the Ethereum Enterprise Alliance, an organization with more than 500 members that develops open blockchain infrastructures to solve enterprise-grade issues.

Perspectives for Hyperledger

Although most Hyperledger's projects are still in the development phase, some companies have started using Sawtooth or Fabric to empower their product or service. Everledger, for instance, which we covered in `Chapter 7`, *Blockchain for the Business World and Achievements*, was designed through Hyperledger Fabric and allows clients, authorities, lawyers, accounts, and every intermediary in the diamond supply chain to transparently track the recording process of diamonds. This reduces jewelry fraud (estimated at millions of dollars) by replacing the paper-based tracking method with a digitized one. And Everledger is not the only player who saw the potential of Hyperledger's projects. Spearheaded by Intel and IBM, their massive client portfolio is starting to pay attention to the opportunities offered by private blockchains. Hyperledger's projects are on the verge of answering an enormous market where the need for collaboration has never been bigger.

All in all, Hyperledger will help to secure and customize supply verifications, logistics, distribution, and payment verifications between entities. Besides Sawtooth and Fabric, which are the most advanced and well-known projects, Hyperledger has taken eight other initiatives under its wing, ranging from an implementation of the Ethereum smart contract engine (Burrow), to a distributed digital identity system (Indy), to an interoperability platform for running transactions across ledgers (Quilt).

Aergo

One emerging project worth mentioning is Blocko's Aergo. Founded in 2014, Blocko is a Korean blockchain company that launched a product in May 2019 called Aergo that provides a network infrastructure for organizations to build and deploy their own blockchain. Aergo aims to become the most widespread architecture for enterprise application developers and to advance its usage to a mass market thanks to a user-friendly interface combined with a simplified administration and pre-built applications. The solution is cloud-based and offers the possibility to create public, private, or semi-private blockchains. Blocko operates in the UK, South Korea, and Hong Kong and has already released 20 systems, utilized by 9 million users worldwide (`https://coinjournal.net/ samsung-backed-startup-blocko-launches-hybrid-blockchain-aergo-enterprise/`). Designed with three different modules, Aergo is a very ambitious product. The first brick is Aergo Chain, a public blockchain infrastructure, basically aiming to outperform Ethereum. Aergo Chain combines an easy way to create smart contracts with a delegated proof-of-stake protocol and the use of sidechains, which largely increase scalability with around one million transactions per second.

The second brick is Aergo Hub, a web-based blockchain hosting service for managing separate independent private blockchains based on Aergo Chain. It can be compared to current cloud-based services with a user-friendly interface for creation, testing, implementation, and maintenance. Aergo Hub also includes Aergo Horde, an orchestration platform to allow multiple blockchains to be installed.

The last brick is Aergo Marketplace, a peer-to-peer trading platform where users can purchase applications, computing resources, or data storage.

In May 2019, Blocko signed an agreement of convergence with Hyundai to build an application for tracking the history of used cars available for purchase including previous owner data, as well as the car's age and mileage. This project is somewhat similar to what Renault is achieving within the MOBI consortium (see `Chapter 7`, *Business for the Blockchain World and Achievements*) with the car's passport relying on an easy-to-use platform for customers. To fulfill their expectations, Blocko raised $8.9 million in its latest funding round in June 2018 and successfully ended its **initial coin offerings** (**ICO**) for Aergo in October 2018 by reaching the $30 million hard cap. Aergo has yet to succeed in bringing about blockchain mass adoption but has so far satisfied and convinced most of the blockchain ecosystem by attempting to build a practical user-friendly blockchain platform.

Corda

Corda is an open source blockchain project specifically designed for business. The main problem Corda is trying to solve is enabling financial institutions, healthcare organizations, and insurance companies to agree simultaneously on the state of their books as well as bringing privacy in transactions between participants of a given consortium. General hurdles in the financial sector affect transaction synchronization and constant truth assessment in account balances through a wide variety of verifications that increase delays and costs for every stakeholder in the process. Corda was built to overcome that by using distributed ledger technology. Corda was developed by R3, a company founded in 2014 that formed a large ecosystem, including financial companies that work together to build applications called CorDapps on the platform.

> "*Corda is a unique, open source platform designed in part to help small entrepreneurs succeed in building solutions for their customer base. Each week we see new and innovative CorDapps being released into different industries.*"
>
> – David Rutter, CEO of R3

The consortium started in September 2015 with nine financial companies to reach, as of January 2019, more than 300 members from private and public sectors, fostered by an important network effect. In contrast to Hyperledger's community that reaches approximately the same size, Corda's members mostly contribute by developing applications and testing the infrastructure. The first app to be developed on Corda was Fusion Lendercomm, a platform for syndicated loans aiming to streamline and digitize information exchange on the market. Through the service, agent banks can easily publish detailed loan information, including credit agreements, accrual balances, position information, and other transaction data, and extend self-service capabilities to lenders. This solution was conjointly developed by R3 itself and Finastra and deployed over seven international banks such as BNP Paribas, HSBC, or Natixis.

Generally speaking, Corda provides its customers with the benefits of public blockchains without the issues of scalability, privacy, and governance, making it more appropriate for enterprises, especially those evolving in highly regulated global markets. Performance and scalability are tough to achieve in a public blockchain because the more nodes that join the network, the lower their throughput rate. User experience tails off accordingly as it takes more time for the nodes to validate and store transactions. Corda chose to focus on privacy and security by properly identifying the nodes through a strong KYC to prevent misbehavior and establish the beginning of trust in the network. This explains why Corda is often considered more of a distributed ledger rather than a blockchain per se. Even though blockchains are a kind of distributed ledger technology, they tend to refer to trustless, highly decentralized, transparent, and barrier-free infrastructures. These are not inner features of Corda, which, however, enables seamless and private value transfer between peers without a supervisory body and succeeds in giving the banking and financial industries a tool they can use to ensure truth and synchronize states between participants:

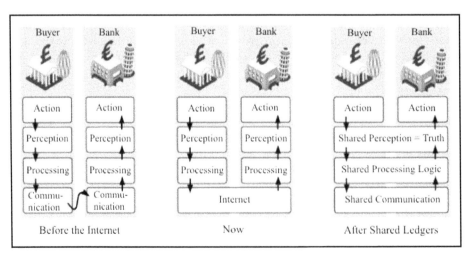

Microsoft Azure

Besides these blockchain infrastructures (Quorum, Hyperledger, Aergo, and Corda), several IT companies started to develop cloud-based solutions to enhance user-friendliness, as well as facilitate setting up a blockchain. Instead of configuring servers and operating maintenance on a specific infrastructure on their own, a decision maker can decide to use a fully integrated service called BaaS. Investopedia defines BaaS as follows:

> *"Blockchain as a Service (BaaS) is an offering that allows customers to leverage cloud-based solutions to build, host and use their own blockchain apps, smart contracts, and functions on the blockchain while the cloud-based service provider manages all the necessary tasks and activities to keep the infrastructure agile and operational."*

As BaaS is gaining momentum in 2019, let's review some of the solutions currently available on the market.

Among the big IT companies, Microsoft is a precursor. In 2014, they started accepting Bitcoin as a payment option to purchase digital content such as apps or games from their Windows Phone and Xbox. They actually published research papers in 2012 about Bitcoin's protocol weaknesses and offered a BaaS solution in 2016 after partnering with ConsenSys, a startup founded by Joseph Lubin, a major supporter of Ethereum. Lately, in May 2019, Microsoft announced the commercialization of Azure Blockchain Service, a product allowing the creation, management, and governance of consortium blockchain networks. Azure Blockchain Service is a fully managed service for companies that want to build and maintain their own distributed ledgers and build applications on it, enabling the definition of permissions, monitoring of activities, and control of participants. This service was launched while a partnership was announced simultaneously with J.P. Morgan to make available its blockchain, Quorum, on Microsoft's platform, hence making it the first usable ledger in Azure Blockchain Service.

AWS

A few days before the launch of Azure Blockchain Service, Amazon announced the general availability of Amazon Managed Blockchain, a service somewhat similar to Microsoft's, enabling the creation and management of scalable blockchains based on open source frameworks such as Hyperledger or, in the future, Ethereum. AWS is the latest cloud service provider to launch a blockchain-related offer, a startling fact regarding Amazon's ability to open up markets for its competitors and benefit from the usual first-mover advantage upon emerging technologies such as IoT or machine learning. This delay was explained by Andy Jassy, AWS's CEO, who deplored, at the end of 2017, the lack of blockchain use cases in production, before turning things around a few months later in April 2018 by launching AWS Blockchain Templates, its first blockchain product, enabling quick private or public network setup. In any case, AWS has caught up with Microsoft in providing an effective solution and today has a decent position in the market, mainly because they were able to benefit from their large user base.

Concretely, with managed Blockchains, users are able to create a network from scratch by inviting members to become nodes and run applications deployed onto the platform. AWS facilitates the establishment of a consortium between companies to transact in a trustless environment and takes charge of the whole maintenance of the network. As a first success, AWS signed a partnership in May 2018 with Kaleido, a platform developed by ConsenSys designed to simplify the erection of a blockchain, to quick-test different use case scenarios.

BaaS solutions such as Amazon's provide great flexibility for setting up and running a blockchain on a given infrastructure because they take responsibility for integrating ongoing evolutions and upgrades. In other words, upgradability and maintenance remain under the supervision of the cloud services provider, leaving you with more room to focus on the go-to-market strategy.

IBM

When IBM joined the Hyperledger movement as a founding corporate member in 2016, it was already working on a blockchain framework that was integrated into the Hyperledger project and became the Fabric module. Original motivations for this initiative came from two observations made by the IBM team:

- Bitcoin and Ethereum are barely scalable due to several drawbacks (an energy-consuming consensus protocol, a growing permissionless network, and an increasing database size).
- Bitcoin and Ethereum do not support private transactions in their core model.

Since IBM spearheads most developments of Hyperledger Fabric by having contributed much of the code, it was expected that their solution called IBM Blockchain unveiled in March 2017 would make use of this specific module. This cloud-based solution enables developers to build robust and effective networks with improved security features including protection from insider attacks and an additional layer cloistering the registry off the cloud. Other components such as a digital identity management tool, a governance tool, and a shut-down option when a piracy attack is identified, are provided with the fully-integrated service. IBM's long-term IT expertise has been leveraged to offer a strong and hack-resistant cloud-based alternative empowered by a large group of developers, intending to offer their clients an easy-to-deploy solution that can support any kind of application. Maersk, Everledger, and Walmart, whose blockchain use cases were discussed in `Chapter 7`, *Blockchain for the Business World and Achievements*, are all leading organizations that have been making use of IBM Blockchain since its early days in 2017. As blockchain is a strategic imperative according to IBM's CEO, Ginni Rometty, IBM took a leap in June 2019 by upgrading its Blockchain platform to enable multi-cloud deployments across hybrid clouds such as AWS and Azure, in order to bring the next level of interoperability and, of course, decentralization.

"Internet was to information what blockchain is to transactions in terms of making them really cheap to record and easy to verify."

– Ginni Rometty, IBM CEO

Oracle

Oracle CEO Mark Hurd declared in 2017, during the OpenWorld convention, that blockchain was the *next big thing* and that it can allow companies to attain their main priorities: increasing revenue, boosting cash flow, decreasing spending, and managing risk. Hurd confirmed these thoughts the following year at the same event, saying that in a supply chain, 65% of the managers manually track the shipment of goods whereas blockchain could provide applications to provide automation and increase security and facilitate information exchange. In these circumstances, Oracle announced, in July 2018, the launch of its own blockchain platform to catch up with IBM's progress. This platform, designed as a service on Oracle Cloud, is called Oracle **Blockchain Cloud Service** (**BCS**), and just like IBM, is built on the Hyperledger Fabric framework. It was adopted by several companies such as CargoSmart (see `Chapter 7`, *Blockchain for the Business World and Achievements*) and the Arab Jordan Investment Bank to help them to move quickly from prototypes to operational products, thanks to a large range of services and support.

> *"We are leveraging blockchain to simplify complex shipping documentation processes and improve customers' operational efficiency by building a collaborative network. Oracle Blockchain Cloud Service enables a shorter application delivery lead time with 30% productivity gains compared to other solutions."*
>
> *– Steve Siu, CargoSmart CEO*

Oracle also provides its clients with integration developments, administration, and core components such as smart contracts development, nodes administration, and storage space. Oracle's BaaS offer allows members to automate day-to-day operations by creating, running, and maintaining on-purpose applications.

Key takeaway

As a decision maker, if you are willing to launch a blockchain project, the choice of the infrastructure has to be carefully examined. Of course, you can develop your own blockchain from scratch, but that would take much more time and many more resources than using an already existing infrastructure. Ethereum, Bitcoin, and other public blockchains are sometimes successful enough depending on your needs. But to unlock certain industrial issues encountered in the business world, you might consider using another solution.

Between Corda, Quorum, Hyperledger, and Aergo, the choice is quite hard. They are all enterprise-ready and open source, supported by growing communities of developers and organizations. Each solution was created to build on-purpose permissioned blockchains as an alternative to slow and hard-to-scale public infrastructures. The few differences we can identify between them revolve around their primary target and vision. While Hyperledger integrates modular frameworks such as Fabric or Sawtooth to suit the needs of several industries from healthcare to energy, Quorum and Corda are mainly finance-oriented. The large span of modules proposed by Hyperledger can get pretty confusing for a newcomer but have the benefit of meeting any kind of need for any kind of industry. Quorum and Corda, on the other hand, focus mainly on privacy and security issues as well as scalability and overall performance to enable a large number of transactions and quasi-instantaneous block creation. User-friendliness comes into the equation as an important criterion for mass adoption in the business world: Aergo, Corda, and Quorum are more accessible solutions than Hyperledger, whose plethora of resources, activities, training courses, events, and projects can become quite overwhelming for a decision maker keen to launch a blockchain project. The following is a short summary and comparison between the infrastructures presented in this chapter:

	Quorum	Hyperledger	Aergo	Corda
Developer	J.P.Morgan (based on Ethereum)	The Linux Foundation and other members	Blocko	R3
Speed	100+ tx/second	3 K+ tx/second	20 K + tx/second	150 = tx/second
Private Blockchain	Yes	Yes	Yes	Yes
Open Source	Yes	Yes	Yes	Yes
Programming Language	Solidity	Java, Golang, NodeJS	SQL, Lua	Java, Kotlin
Token	Ether	None	Aergo	None

Cloud-based solutions provide the ability to easily install a node or a server from a template and set up the configuration of the network. Even though your company benefits from a large skilled team of developers, they might not be confident enough to embrace the ownership and maintenance of blockchain infrastructure. Moreover, as many companies already use cloud-based services for other needs, it might seem more suitable to extend the agreement to BaaS and benefit from outsourcing maintenance and backend development. Another advantage in using BaaS solutions is that the technology evolves very rapidly and it can become cumbersome to handle the integration of upgrades and patches, as well as resolve scalability issues that can be left upto the service provider. Because these solutions are *as a service*, the provider takes over maintaining the servers and monitoring and managing the network. However, as a decision maker, you must challenge every solution you choose and focus on how decentralized it actually is. Indeed, if you determined that a blockchain was the most suitable tool to answer your needs, it implies that the state of the digital value must be ascertained without a central entity, in a decentralized manner. Choosing a BaaS might sometimes go against the inner purpose of a blockchain, which is enabling decentralization, because the nodes are usually hosted on the same provider's servers:

Editor	Launch date	Technical aspects	References
Microsoft's Azure Blockchain Service	January 2016	Supports Quorum and Corda	J.P.Morgan, Nasdaq, 3M
AWS Managed Blockchain	April 2018	Supports Hyperledger and Ethereum	Nestle, Singapore Exchange
IBM Blockchain Platform	March 2017	Supports Hyperledger	Everledger, Mistubishi
Oracle Blockchain Cloud Service	July 2018	Supports Hyperledger	CargoSmart

In any case, instead of setting up and running a blockchain from scratch, companies can now outsource the technical work and focus on developing applications and smart contracts, a better alternative for taking your first step in the ecosystem to understand how the technology works and quickly try out proof-of-concepts. Even though the market is still emerging, many infrastructures and cloud-based products have appeared over the past few years, leaving you with enough choice to overcome any business issue identified in your industry or organization.

Summary

This chapter started by illustrating the evolution of blockchains and by exploring its different designs: public, private, and semi-private. We then covered some of the most mature solutions on the market such as Hyperledger or Corda, but also the most promising ones such as Quorum and Aergo. We also reviewed cloud-based solutions that provide enterprise-grade platforms to extend business processes and applications, and eventually understood why these solutions have to be handled cautiously to remain consistent with blockchain principles.

In the next chapter, we will harness different strategic approaches to implementing a blockchain and explore the various points that have to be considered when launching a blockchain project. We will cover important features that, as a decision maker, must be grasped properly in the global path toward building a *digital-ready* enterprise.

10
Defining Your Needs

According to IBM, C-suite executives tend to be very cautious toward disruptive business technologies, mainly because they trigger a much cheaper and faster market entrance for new companies, hence strengthening competition. On the other hand, it is no secret that many businesses collapse due to their inadaptability to meet evolving demands, especially in the digital age. In the latest PwC CEO Survey (`https://www.pwc.com/gx/en/ceo-survey/2019/report/pwc-22nd-annual-global-ceo-survey.pdf`), 28% of businesses have rated speed of technological change as an extremely concerning threat. Often, these traditional companies occult the fact that digitalization has quickly shifted the way products and services are consumed and struggle to leverage new technology to answer new consumption behaviors from clients and prospects. Blockchain is not going to make it easier for companies showing inertia on their path toward digitalization. Blockchain will not only contribute to changing consumption habits but it will also change how data flows and how value is transferred between economic actors, reshaping the capitalist economy in a more collaborative and transparent system where value is shared in a more horizontal manner. In this fashion, companies have a strong challenge ahead in developing a certain level of knowledge toward blockchain to avoid being sidelined in the coming years. But where can we start? In this chapter, we will approach a method to starting a blockchain project, address the risks and opportunities that have to be taken into consideration, the underlying and inevitable costs, and finally, the traps that must be avoided.

In this chapter, we will cover the following topics:

- A pragmatic reasoning
- How much does a blockchain cost?
- Challenges and issues
- Business leaders' perception of blockchain

Deciding to implement a blockchain

Any organization should start with a problem statement. Starting from the technology is pointless because it does not answer the end user's need. I often compare this typical behavior as grabbing a screwdriver and checking what can be fixed with it. Sure, some stuff might be repaired along the way, but the main problem would not have been fixed. Hence, it is important to identify the problem first, before thinking of a way out.

Once the issue has been identified, you should focus on the simplest solution available and answer the question: *Do I actually need a blockchain?*

The final response to this question will most likely be determined by the subsequent questions:

- Do you need to ensure a state of information or allow a digital value to be transferred between stakeholders?
- Are all of the stakeholders independent?
- Is there any trust tying the stakeholders?
- Is there a common interest in collaborating and sharing information?

These are probably the most important questions to raise, although a decision tree might be more helpful:

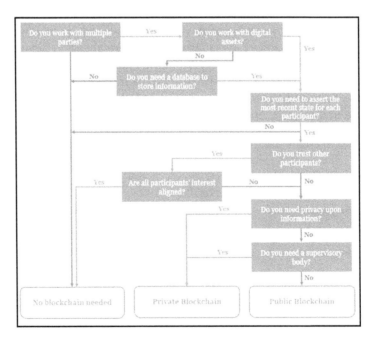

If blockchain is relevant, then you should assess the potential impact of the project with a business case, which is the first requirement in any IT project. The business case should include a variety of issues, such as how regulatory constraints are addressed, how many resources are needed, which standards should be used and implemented and, of course, what needs does the final product or service answer to. A way to push the assessment further is to analyze the firm's acceptance level of change and the risk tolerance level. Based on these outputs, it will become easier to determine a rational **return on investment** (**ROI**) to decide whether to invest. By identifying the potential gain according to the risk-reward premise, you will be able to thoroughly establish a strategic approach for your project and, more broadly, for your company.

Before launching a blockchain project, you should also ensure that all stakeholders are aligned and that strong governance is in place, that is defining the roles and responsibilities of everyone in the network so that you can properly design the infrastructure. A blockchain's success mostly lies in the nodes' independency. One node should be sovereign over its decision to validate transaction and information storage; that is why governance is a real issue when it comes to blockchain. Do not forget that this is the network that empowers the blockchain; hence, this is probably the most important component to deal with.

Only then should focus be made on the design of the solution and the choice of the infrastructure. The proof-of-concept phase is very important because the technology is evolving at a rapid pace and a concrete demonstration is very useful for picturing the product and quantify the benefits. Evolving as an agile enterprise with continuous improvement and incremental releases is key to adapting to customers' needs. In the meantime, the enterprise should put in place the necessary organizational frameworks, including working groups and communication processes, so that development, integration, production, and adoption are sufficiently supported. Eventually, taking care of finance, marketing, and commerce will become mandatory if we want to be able to deliver the project as well as being assured that sufficient economic and technological support is provided.

To help you build your roadmap and business case, the following is a list of items to address that may be used to keep your blockchain project on track:

	Items	Expectations
Business	Problem	Describe the problem you are trying to solve
	Solution	Describe the solution that will solve the problem
Structure	Participants	Define the number of participants, their industry, size, interests and current mode of operation
	Network	Describe the role and the rights of the nodes, the validators and the users
	Incentive	Define the motivation the validators within the network have to ensure the truth / If applicable, define the typology and economics of the token
Procedure	Transaction	Explain the kind of transactions happening on the network and the kind of value being shared
	Protocol	Describe the consensus and the rules in place for validating the transactions

Now that you've learned about whether or not to implement a blockchain project in your organization, let's find out how much a blockchain project can cost.

How much does a blockchain cost?

You probably won't be surprised if I tell you that the price of a blockchain project varies a lot. Depending on what you are willing to achieve, the use of a certain infrastructure over another will range the investments from small to large. For example, the cost of authenticating official documents through a public blockchain will mostly comprise the transaction fees levied by the network to process the transactions, which is not a very expensive blockchain application. Using a public blockchain is sometimes the cheapest solution if we wish to benefit from an already existing infrastructure. Besides the transaction fees, the costs will mostly rely on developing the application on top of it and focusing on user experience.

On the other hand, if you are building an entire network from scratch, like Facebook is doing with their Libra Project where they create a permissioned blockchain integrating smart contracts based on a new programming language, it might involve a greater deal of money. What will mostly make the total cost vary is the size of the network powering the infrastructure and how many users will be exploiting the service. Scaling up a permissioned blockchain to an inter-enterprise level can become very expensive.

In general, a blockchain project varies from $5,000 for identifying and defining a complete use case to $200,000 for an industrialized solution. Knowing that a blockchain developer costs between $500 and $900 a day, you might consider outsourcing these services to external companies whose prices are much lower, although distance can become a negative factor for the execution of the project. This downside can be, however, offset by eliminating a difficult task from the roadmap: building a multi-skill profiles team with R&D researchers, data analysts, business analysts, and developers. It is important to note that solely engaging blockchain experts will not help you to achieve an end-to-end process.

All in all, there is a trade-off to finding, building or choosing the best suitable blockchain: its functionality, its transaction speed, the security level, its consensus mechanism, and the degree of centralization. In short, the costs for deploying a blockchain will depend mostly on the following:

- The functionalities chosen to run the infrastructure
- The velocity of transactions
- The complexity of the chosen consensus protocol
- The type of blockchain (public, private, or semi-private)
- The size of the network (nodes and validators)

If you choose a cloud-based solution (with Microsoft, AWS, IBM, or Oracle, for example) the development costs can shrink quickly while subscription and maintenance fees heighten. For a first blockchain project, these solutions sound more appropriate because it provides flexibility and more room for manoeuvring when iterating on the final product or service. As I stated previously, attention is required for cloud-based solutions; however, the degree of decentralization can be reduced to zero for some providers offering solutions that are hosted on their own servers. This kind of infrastructure actually eliminates the prime interest in implementing a blockchain because it creates a single point of failure and erases the nodes' independency.

As of June 2019, the market is very fragmented and it can be confusing for decision makers to select the best option. The more companies start paying attention to blockchain, the more blockchain platforms are emerging and the less likely that one actor emerges from the crowd. Despite growing live product and media coverage, no one can tell which infrastructure is going to thrive between public and permissioned blockchains. However, there are decent solutions on the market already, such as Ethereum or Hyperledger, which benefit from large financial support.

Regarding the conduct of an ICO, most of the costs will comprise data privacy compliance such as completing KYC and AML policies, and marketing strategy such as white paper redaction, bounty programs (bounty programs are incentives offered during an ICO to social media influencers, blog writers, and video makers to help democratize the project and spread the word), and communication plans. Additional fees can also be added regarding external expertise for the ICO, such as the typology of the token and tokenomics (tokenomics is a combination of the words *token* and *economics*. This is about the economic choices that are made to build the project's token, such as the ecosystem, the business model, the usage, the legal side, or the technological structure.).

Challenges and issues

Now that you have every key to carry out a blockchain project, you must be aware of some shortcomings that are usually encountered with traditional blockchain project management and operations that might curb your initiative:

- Stakeholders' processes vary widely according to the organization and even more according to the industry.
- Many differences exist between stakeholders' systems for managing operations and running projects.
- Organizations often use disparate tools between their own departments or services, which does not facilitate traceability and smoothness during implementation. Because these departments usually run operations in silos, there is a lack of a wider approach where the processes would be integrated, transparent, and interoperable.

These issues make data management difficult, increase cost, and extend delays, hence leading to a loss in both quality and user experience triggered by inefficiencies across the process. If you are willing to use blockchain to meet customers' expectations as well as enhance a product or a process, you really should consider addressing the aforementioned issues by raising awareness with all of the stakeholders and achieving a strong market study, as well as selecting a proper IT infrastructure. This goes along with assessing the level of *competition* of the network, that is, assessing how sensitive the data is and the value that will be shared between the stakeholders who are likely to provide someone with a competitive advantage. You must analyze whether the project, once deployed, will bring greater benefit to end users rather than to some participants of the network.

Companies in commercial food, carrier, automotive, or luxury goods are working on a *competitive* background with the common purpose of bringing added value to the customers despite their ongoing competition. For that matter, keep in mind that blockchain unleashes possibilities for companies to jointly undertake actions with others in a trustless environment and should not provide a competitive advantage to one or several participants because it can lead to a loss of independency that hinders the assessment of truth within the network.

In any case, from initialization to industrialization, a project is not straightforward. Even though most of the solutions out there are open source and allow enablers to help you quickly understand mining and smart contracts, for example, there are inevitable steps along the way. Adopting a wider approach, the first step would be to choose the platform. Note that Ethereum generally makes unanimity and has been chosen by many companies for their project because of its dynamism and its large supporting community and rich documentation. Once the platform has been chosen, you have to initialize the blockchain, that is, create nodes and trigger the first block, including the choice of data velocity, transaction timespan, and the size of the blocks. This step can be outsourced to service providers who will take care of setup and configuration. Eventually, the choice of the consensus protocol rises and will depend on whether your project includes a certain degree of confidentiality and restrictions (in other words, a private network) or if you have chosen a public blockchain. As we mentioned previously, the use of proof-of-work within private networks is irrelevant because the nodes are identified and they do not need to compete based on computational power. As a last step, you must deploy your applications and smart contracts, remaining careful of the programming language that was used to develop them after having checked whether it is handled by the service provider. Do not forget that the application itself is why you wrote a business case and chose blockchain in the first place. Needless to say, your final product must convenience end users; otherwise, why choose blockchain?

Business leaders' perception of blockchain

This chapter aims to establish the key statements and perceptions of business leaders and executives around the world. It is often interesting to hear the opinion of other people, especially those who influence and stimulate our vision. An emerging technology usually raises critics among economists, scientists, and politicians debating financial, ethical, environmental, social, or technical benefits and drawbacks.

Over the past few years, blockchain has attracted a growing community of developers, businessmen, scientists, and tech-savvy people who contributed to democratizing the technology and exposing its applicability. But the ecosystem has also faced several critics and disbeliefs, sometimes from tech leaders or people who actually led the advancement of the technology in the first place. Criticism started to rise as blockchain was gaining popularity. Starting from 2017, blockchain underwent massive media coverage due to the rise in the price of Bitcoin and other cryptocurrencies. Research regarding the word **blockchain** occurred 3.7 million times in 2017 and 500,000 articles were written that year about this topic.

Blockchain in discussion

Back in 2015 in Davos, during the World Economic Forum, blockchain was first mentioned as one of the six mega-trends that would contribute to the transition to a more digital and connected world. The report asserting this estimation was based on a survey of more than 800 IT executives and experts and was conducted by the Global Agenda Council on the Future of Software and Society. It was estimated that, by 2027, 10% of the global GDP will be stored on blockchain (`http://www3.weforum.org/docs/WEF_GAC15_Technological_Tipping_Points_report_2015.pdf`) and will have important impacts on financial inclusion in emerging markets, tradable assets, property records, and exchangeable services and value. This was a very bold prediction at the time, by Victoria Espinel, president and CEO of the Business Software Alliance, a trade group representing the world's largest software makers, such as Kaspersky Lab and whose mission is to prevent copyright infringement of software. There's no doubt that her report was very clairvoyant as she added a conclusion that, if blockchain came to be widely adopted, governments would need to rethink their traditional mode of operation and the way they function.

Espinel's report sharply contrasts with statements that were made the previous year at the same event. Invited to Davos, the US Treasury Secretary, Jack Lew expressed his incredulity toward Bitcoin, declaring that he was making sure that it will not be used to finance illegal activities that have malign purposes. This declaration was a blatant confession of his misunderstanding of Bitcoin and blockchain. In fact, the decentralized infrastructure of Bitcoin prevents any authority from taking over the network and controlling the way value is transferred between individuals. Unfortunately, because of that, Bitcoin has been used as a means to purchase illicit products, but that was mainly true until the online global drug bazaar, Silk Road, was shut down (`https://www.wired.com/2015/04/silk-road-1/`).

Not long after Jack Lew's declaration, J.P. Morgan's CEO, Jamie Dimon, followed the same vein, stating that his company had nothing to do with Bitcoin because law enforcement will eventually put an end to it. Ironically, J.P. Morgan is now a leading actor in the cryptosphere and has launched its own tokens, JPM Coin, and its own blockchain infrastructure, Quorum. This stark turnaround happened less than two years after Jamie Dimon called Bitcoin a fraud and threatened to fire any analyst that was trading it. This is a quite intriguing behavior to say the least, especially because Umar Farooq, Global Head of Blockchain at J.P. Morgan, gave a totally different speech about the technology:

> *"We have always believed in the potential of blockchain and we are supportive of cryptocurrencies as long as they are properly controlled and regulated. As a globally regulated bank, we believe we have a unique opportunity to develop the capability in a responsible way with the oversight of our regulators."*

Back in 2014, Dimon's declarations inspired a reaction from Virgin's famous founder, Sir Richard Branson. In an interview with CNBC, the billionaire entrepreneur claimed that there will be, in the coming years, a global digital currency that will take on banks and other traditional currencies (`https://www.cnbc.com/2014/01/24/branson-on-bitcoin-take-that-mr-dimon.html`). Branson also took advantage of this interview to announce that tickets for his commercial space flight, Virgin Galactic, could be purchased with Bitcoin, which made it one of the first international business to accept Bitcoin as a means of payment.

Since then, water has flowed under the bridge and more blockchain advocates have had their voice heard. One of the most well-known is probably Don Tapscott. This Canadian business executive and consultant dedicated his life to supporting companies and their business strategies and the role of technology in their growth path. In 2017, Tapscott founded the Blockchain Research Institute, a renowned independent global think-tank currently helping more than a hundred projects study the implications of blockchain on businesses, governments, and society. According to Tapscott, blockchain should not be compared to any other new technologies such as AI, big data, or the **Internet of Things (IoT)** but rather as the trigger initiating the fourth industrial revolution, the layer that will allow all-new technologies to transact autonomously in an entirely digital world.

In contrast to the optimistic posture of Don Tapscott stands the toughest detractor of blockchain that could be found, that is, Nouriel Roubini, who declared on January 25, 2019 that blockchain was no better than an Excel spreadsheet. The economist, who predicted the 2008 economic crisis, also defined blockchain as the most overhyped technology ever.

Besides throwing rocks in the lake, Roubini believes that digital currencies backed by central banks do not have anything to do with blockchain nor cryptocurrencies because they are centrally governed by a single entity. This statement was surprisingly well received by the blockchain ecosystem as it proved that, besides Roubini's ominous point of view, he is actually well aware of the blockchain's intrinsic values.

High profile opinions

I could keep on illustrating different opinions from different leaders across the globe, describing every positive, negative, surprising, deceiving, or encouraging statement that blockchain has mooted since the creation of Bitcoin in 2009, but figures have more to say than one thousand words.

Check out the following IT/digital/innovation executives and leaders:

	Name	Organization	Notable position	Perception towards Blockchain	Statement
	Don Tapscott	Blockchain Research Institute	Chairman	Advocate	To be sure, the blockchain provides opportunities to stop the stampede to a surveillance society
	Bill Gates	Microsoft	Founder		As an asset class, you're not producing anything and so you shouldn't expect it to go up. It's kind of a pure 'greater fool theory' type of investment
	Richard Branson	Virgin	Founder		Virgin Galactic is a bold entrepreneurial technology. It's driving a revolution. And Bitcoin is doing just the same when it comes to inventing a new currency
	Eric Schmidt	Alphabet	Chairman		[Bitcoin] is a remarkable cryptographic achievement. The ability to create something which is not duplicable in the digital world has enormous value. Lot's of people will build businesses on top of that
	Peter Thiel	Paypal	Cofounder		Paypal had these goals of creating a new currency. We failed at that, and we just created a new payment system. I think Bitcoin has succeeded on the level of a new currency
	Mark Hurd	Oracle	CEO		Blockchain's promise is the fact that it can help bring sets of data from different variable applications and [make] it secure
	David Furlonger	Gartner	VP		It is critical to understand what blockchain is and what it is capable of today, compared to how it will transform companies, industries and society tomorrow

Among banking/investment executives and leaders, we have the following:

	Name	Organization	Notable position	Perception towards Blockchain	Statement
	Jamie Dimon	J.P. Morgan	CEO	Whoops	I don't give a sh*t about Bitcoin
	Lloyd Blankfein	Goldman Sachs	CEO		If you could go through that fiat currency where they say this is worth what it's worth because I, the government, says it is, why couldn't you have a consensus currency?
	Warren Buffet	Berkshire Hathaway	CEO	Detractor	Stay away from [Bitcoin]. It's a mirage, basically. In terms of cryptocurrencies, generally, I can say almost with certainty that they will come to a bad ending
	Tim Sloan	Wells Fargo	CEO		Blockchain has been way oversold. I think the fundamental technology is very interesting, but it's been very slow to roll out

Among economists, we have the following:

	Name	Organization	Notable position	Perception towards Blockchain	Statement
	Nouriel Roubini	RGE Monitor	Founder	Detractor	Blockchain isn't about democracy and decentralization, it's about greed
	Alan Greenspan	US Federal Reserve	Former Chairman	Favorite	Bitcoin is what used to be called fiat money
	Joseph Stiglitz	Columbia University	Professor and Nobel Prize	Detractor	I actually think we should shut down the cryptocurrencies

Among public institutions executives and leaders, we have the following:

	Name	Organization	Notable position	Perception towards Blockchain	Statement
	Arunma Oteh	World Bank	Treasurer		[Talking about a blockchain product launched by the World Bank] I am delighted that this pioneer bond transaction using the distributed ledger technology, bond-i, was extremely well received by investors
	Mario Draghi	European Central Bank	Chairman	Adverse	Cryptocurrencies or bitcoins, or anything like that, are not really currencies, they are assets. A euro is a euro, today, tomorrow, in a month, it's always a euro. And the ECB is behind the euro. Who is behind the cryptocurrencies? So they are very, very risky assets.
	Christina Lagarde	International Monetary Fund	Chairwoman		I believe we should consider the possibility to issue digital currency. There may be a role for the state to supply money to the digital economy.
	Roberto Azevedo	World Trade Organization	Chairman		While this technology opens interesting opportunities, clearly it also raises legal, regulatory and policy issues that deserve our attention. We need to consider how to spread the opportunities and overcome the challenges.
	Jerome Powell	US Federal Reserve	Chairman		Almost no one uses bitcoin for payments, they use it more as an alternative to gold

As you can see, opinions are very divergent according to the executive's background, industry, position, and nationality. Obviously, leaders from the IT sector seem to have a propensity to support blockchain and cryptocurrencies more than their peers in the financial industry, although some of them remain cautious about how to actually reach production-level applicability and broad market acceptance. Among economists, the debate stays wide open, especially regarding the economic concepts and social theories blockchain involves. For public institutions leaders, it is important to notice that the topic has not yet been investigated, although the World Bank took a great leap by issuing $108 million of blockchain-based bonds on a private version of Ethereum in August 2018. All in all, blockchain and cryptocurrencies have been discussed extensively within different business areas and between major executives.

Summary

Throughout this chapter, we've underlined that identifying and understanding the business problem is the key to solving it because it's the best starting point on which to build a successful solution. We showed that, sometimes, blockchain was not appropriate because the solution didn't involve criteria that was mandatory when choosing blockchain, such as the need to store information or the alignment of participants' interests. But when blockchain stands as a suitable solution, many diverse assessments, requirements, and topics must be addressed. Among them is the return on investment, the regulatory constraints, or the acceptance level of the teams to change. Besides these open points, we tried to answer a difficult but necessary question regarding the cost of a blockchain, which, in the end, can be considered a regular IT project including specific features, especially when it comes to launching an ICO. Then, we discussed challenges and issues that must be taken into consideration, such as the consensus protocol, the degree of competition in the network, and data management. Eventually, we illustrated some opinions and statements from business executives and leaders worldwide and showed how diverse the perception of blockchain is between economists, politics, technologists, and managers.

As a global conclusion of this book, the key takeaway is that blockchain, just like big data, artificial intelligence or Internet-of-Things should be considered as an enabler and not as a goal. This book demonstrated all the keys for a decision maker or any curious business person to grasp this new technology, to understand its application and all the stakes gravitating around it. It was reinforced that blockchain was not a solution to every business issue, but rather an emerging computing infrastructure enabling digital value to be exchanged in a peer-to-peer manner without any trusted third party. With that in mind, the extent of the disruption in the current economy system that blockchain could bring was illustrated. The goal was not to praise blockchain, but rather set out all of its characteristics and successful stories we have witnessed in the last few years.

I would like to recall that the purpose of a company in the digital age is not to build decentralized ledgers, connected objects or powerful algorithms. Companies are not judged by customers nor investors on how many digital solutions they have deployed, how much money they have spent to become digital-ready, or how responsive to change they are. Instead, a company is supposed to be able to answer specific business issues, reach specific business goals as well as cater to customers' needs in order to prosper in the digital age and keep growing profitably. As a decision maker it is important not to confound means and aims, that is, be able to draw a distinction between the objectives and the tools that will help you fulfill them. Innovation in general is one of those tools.

The path to becoming an innovative organization can be defined in four steps. First, a focus should be made on standardization, that is on simplifying and documenting processes. Standardization does not involve any digital solutions and is only the precise description of processes and stakeholders. Second, the pursuit of dematerialization through digitization of paper-based processes will put the organization ready for disruption. Third, industrialization that often comes along with dematerialization enables reaching a continuous pace of production through the implementation of methods within the processes. Last but not least, implementing innovative tools as a final layer (whether it is robots, algorithms or blockchain) will help you increase speed, lessen risks and increase reliability. This mindset should be embraced by every C-Level executive willing to implement a new technology in their organization, because it requires patience and a strong willingness to transform. Blockchain is no exception, especially regarding its newness and difficulty to apprehend.

Throughout this book we explored how it works, what it is composed of, what economic and legal challenges it embarks, how it is implemented and tackled by leading organizations, and how it could be deployed. I truly hope that you now have a better understanding of this emerging technology to the point that you have grasped enough aspects to form your own opinion of blockchain. I also hope that you developed enough interest to keep an eye on its future, and of course that you could go on to explain it to your teams, colleagues, relatives or friends. As a final takeaway, here is an elevator pitch of what a blockchain is:

Basically, blockchain takes the form of a database which is:

- **Decentralized**: It is not owned by anyone, no one is proprietary of the ledger
- **Shared**: This database is distributed across all the network, everyone owns a copy of the ledger up-to-date
- **Transparent**: Anyone in the network can bring up the history of the ledger and see what happened in the past, which transactions have been validated and when
- **Secured**: Every transaction or information happening on the network is validated in a consensual manner and stored in the ledger thanks to cryptographic algorithms

With a more technical approach, a blockchain is a distributed ledger combining three main technologies:

- **A peer-to-peer network**: Computers are connected to each other through internet and exchange information
- **A consensus mechanism**: Computers across the network agree to adding information to the ledger, thanks to a protocol that allows common agreement in a network where less than 50% of it is dishonest
- **Cryptography**: Algorithms are run to ensure the ledger's security, where every transaction or information validated are immutable

Other Books You May Enjoy

If you enjoyed this book, you may be interested in these other books by Packt:

Blockchain By Example

Bellaj Badr, Richard Horrocks and Xun (Brian) Wu

ISBN: 978-1-78847-568-6

- Grasp decentralized technology fundamentals to master blockchain principles
- Build blockchain projects on Bitcoin, Ethereum, and Hyperledger
- Create your currency and a payment application using Bitcoin
- Implement decentralized apps and supply chain systems using Hyperledger
- Write smart contracts, run your ICO, and build a Tontine decentralized app using Ethereum
- Implement distributed file management with blockchain
- Integrate blockchain into existing systems in your organization

Blockchain for Business 2019
Peter Lipovyanov

ISBN: 978-1-78995-602-3

- Understand the fundamentals of blockchain and how it was developed
- Gain a good understanding of economic concepts and developments
- Develop a base for concepts such as cryptography, computer networking, and programming
- Understand the applications of blockchain and its potential impact on the world
- Become well versed with the latest developments in the blockchain space
- Explore blockchain frameworks, including decentralized organizational structures, networks, and applications

Leave a review - let other readers know what you think

Please share your thoughts on this book with others by leaving a review on the site that you bought it from. If you purchased the book from Amazon, please leave us an honest review on this book's Amazon page. This is vital so that other potential readers can see and use your unbiased opinion to make purchasing decisions, we can understand what our customers think about our products, and our authors can see your feedback on the title that they have worked with Packt to create. It will only take a few minutes of your time, but is valuable to other potential customers, our authors, and Packt. Thank you!

Index

www.ingramcontent.com/pod-product-compliance
Lightning Source LLC
Chambersburg PA
CBHW080530060326
40690CB00022B/5080